MW01109363

Keep being a
difference-Maker!

THE BUSINESS LEADER'S IMPACT

Five Critical Drivers
of
Sustainable Profitable Growth

BY DAN COUGHLIN

Foreword by Lee Renz,
McDonald's USA, Central Division President

Bookbaby
Portland, Oregon

© Dan Coughlin 2014. All rights reserved. No part of this book may be used or reproduced in any manner whatsoever without written permission except in the case of brief quotations embodied in critical articles and reviews.

Bookbaby Publishing

ISBN 978-1-61927-561-4

To Mom and Dad,
the two leaders who had the greatest impact on my life

CONTENTS

I met Dan Coughlin when I was Director of Operations in one of our geographic regions. At that time my strength was in technical expertise, operational initiatives, and talent development. I felt I needed to enhance my ability to influence larger groups of people in multiple departments and in our restaurants as well as our franchisees and suppliers.

Over a period of five years I worked very closely with Dan as he was my executive coach. During that time I was named Vice-President/ General Manager of two different regions for McDonald's. From there I led the McCafé beverage initiative and then moved on to become Chief Restaurant Officer for McDonald's USA.

Today I am President of McDonald's USA's Central Division. In this role I am responsible for over 4,400 restaurants covering 24 states and seven geographic regions.

For five solid years Dan Coughlin and I either met in person or talked over the phone at a minimum of once a month. He would simply ask me about the business, and I would share with him a variety of situations I was facing and aspirations I had for our business results. Dan would always calmly listen until I was done, and then he would start to ask very practical questions like, "What's your single biggest challenge right now?" or "If you could change or improve one thing right now that you think would have the greatest positive impact on moving the business result forward, what would it be and why do you feel that way?"

He listened to my answers, and as I talked he took notes. Then he would summarize his suggestions into a simple, practical process that I could try over the next few weeks. At the next phone call, we would review how the process worked for me and then we would tweak it until it was just what I needed for my situation. Over those five years we developed a wide range of very simple processes that I have used many, many times. As the Division President I have explained many times to top performers at McDonald's how to use the thought processes that Dan taught me.

Our topics seemed to have no limit. We talked about strategy and tactics and people situations and the need to be patient in sticking with a plan even when the desired results weren't pouring in right away and much, much more. We talked about the importance of staying focused and how to strengthen my ability to be creative. Looking back now, the scope of what we dove into was extraordinary.

Most importantly, every idea we discussed was concentrated directly on real business situations to drive real business results. We never sat there and discussed ideas just for the sake of having a discussion. Here are three of my favorite suggestions from Dan.

The Power of Open-ended Questions

Sometimes I simply ask an employee, "How will your suggestion help us to accomplish the goal?" This produces a rich dialogue to verify if the person really understands what's necessary to make progress.

To engage others I'll ask different people in a group, "How did you land on that solution? What was the situation? What needs to be done now? What else did you consider before deciding on what you are proposing?" Now everyone is engaged in the thought process to understand the recommendation.

Develop Solution Leaders

This is about using all the brain power in the room versus just those who choose to contribute. It begins with asking, "What are you trying to achieve?" and "How does it fit with our plan?" Then ask, "Who do you need to influence to get this accomplished?" Listen and no matter what the person says, ask him or her to say more. That way you can verify they have thought this through. Then ask, "How will you know if it is working?" and finally, "What do you need from me?"

The Coach's Card

One day we were discussing a situation where I found myself needing a play. As I talked about this, Dan asked me to say more. I said when you watch football on television the coach has this card full of plays to choose from depending on the situation. He surveys the field and selects the play to run. I told Dan that I find myself in the same situation at times.

Dan went back to his office and created The Coach's Card, which had on it several of the processes that we had developed together. Now as I listen and survey the field in a business situation, I pick a play, or process in this case, from The Coach's Card to use. The beauty here is you can list the steps in every process you develop with Dan and have them on one page. Mine is double-sided and laminated. It contains 13 of the most effective processes we developed together. I use it all the time.

To me, Dan Coughlin has proven his ability to teach ideas where they matter the most: in real-life business situations where people have to deliver strong results day after day. Dan's suggestions are clear, simple, and remarkably useful in actually moving results forward in a positive and successful way.

I've read a lot of business books, but what makes *The Business Leader's Impact* different than the others is that Dan is suggesting ideas to you that have proven to work well not just at McDonald's, but in a wide range of other companies as well. He focuses on the essential aspects of being a successful executive: leadership, teamwork, execution, innovation, and branding. This isn't a book about the technical aspects of your job. This is a very practical book about your ability to lead in a way that will most directly impact your business results in the short term and over the long term.

I encourage you to read Dan's suggestions carefully, try them out in your actual business situations, and then reflect on what changes you can make to his approaches to make them even better for you and your situation. Remember: the key is to improve results, not follow a recipe. Be willing to step back and adjust the processes Dan is suggesting so they become your own. That's what I did when I worked with Dan, and he encouraged me to do so. Then you will truly own the approaches you are using.

Get ready to bring your passion in using these processes and make a great impact in your organization. Good luck on your business journey.

Lee Renz
President
McDonald's USA, Central Division

The Greatest Challenge Businesses Face All Over the World

The greatest challenge that businesses all over the world are facing right now is not to achieve success. We all know of individuals, groups, and organizations who have achieved amazing success just since the turn of the century back in 2000. However, many times these people achieved incredible results only to fall way, way back down. The greatest business challenge isn't to achieve success. The greatest challenge is to achieve success and to sustain that success over the long term.

In essence, the objective is to generate sustainable profitable growth. To do this an organization has to gain and maintain a competitive advantage that matters deeply to customers. This competitive advantage may very well evolve over time and shift into a new direction, but whatever it evolves to it still has to resonate with customers.

That phrase "gain and maintain a competitive advantage that matters deeply to customers" is very easy to type and very hard to accomplish. In having worked with executives at a variety of companies including McDonald's, Marriott, Coca-Cola, Toyota, Abbott, Shell, St. Louis Cardinals, Anheuser-Busch InBev, and RE/MAX, I have come to realize that there are five critical drivers of a competitive advantage that generates sustainable profitable growth for every business. They are leadership, teamwork, execution, innovation, and branding.

I believe that success for an organization begins with effective leadership. An effective leader gets a group of individuals to work together as a team toward achieving meaningful outcomes. The leader and the team establish a plan that when executed well produces the desired results. However, the team has to constantly create more appropriate value for customers through innovation. Ultimately, the organization thrives by earning a brand that is highly valued by customers.

In the absence of any of these five drivers an organization will struggle to maintain its competitive advantage, and this will weaken the organization's ability to sustain profitable growth. This book provides practical advice on strengthening each of these five business drivers.

Dan Coughlin
St. Louis, MO

Accelerate Your Impact as a Business Leader

To me, leadership means influencing how other people think so they make decisions that improve results in a sustainable way. Leadership is not about title, income, or authority. It's also not about gender, race, height, size, or personality type. I've never seen a label that guaranteed a person would be an effective or an ineffective leader. A sustainable competitive advantage that matters deeply to customers doesn't just fall out of the sky. It is crafted into a reality first and foremost by individuals who influence how other people think. These are the leaders in an organization. These are the people who impact the present and the future of the organization. In this chapter we will focus on a variety of key aspects of effective business leadership.

SEE THE ENORMOUS IMPACT OF VALUE AND VALUES

Several years ago I had a meeting in Libertyville, Illinois, which is about 45 miles northwest of Chicago. The meeting started at 8 AM. The day before the meeting I drove from my home in St. Louis to Libertyville, which is a 330-mile drive. If you're wondering why in the world I drove 330 miles as opposed to flying, I just have two words for you: O'Hare Airport. Enough said.

When I was 150 miles into my journey a really important business question popped into my head: I did pack my jacket and my shirt for the meeting tomorrow, didn't I? I looked over my right shoulder and saw that my jacket and shirt were not hanging there. I looked over my left shoulder and noticed the same thing. I had managed to leave my jacket and my shirt in my closet in St. Louis. I drove for five more miles and realized it was too late in the day for me to drive all the way back to St. Louis and make it to Libertyville at a decent hour, and I knew the meeting started too early in the morning for me to get to a department store before it began. After going five more miles, I landed on the only logical solution

I could think of. I called Nordstrom's, the one on Michigan Avenue in downtown Chicago.

I had never been to the Nordstrom's on Michigan Avenue before that night, but I called them up and said, "My name is Dan Coughlin, and I left my jacket and shirt in St. Louis. Is there any possibility you could get a jacket and shirt pressed and ready tonight for me to wear to a meeting tomorrow morning?"

The man said, "I don't think this will be a problem. What size do you wear?"

I said, "42 regular."

He said, "No problem at all. What time will you get here?"

I said, "I think it will be about 9:30."

He said, "Now we have a problem. Our store closes at 9 PM." He paused and then said, "I tell you what. We'll keep our store open for you. When you get here, just come on upstairs and we'll be all ready for you."

I said, "You'll do what?

He said, "Yeah, it's not a problem. When you get here, we'll be all set."

I called two more times for directions. I pulled into the parking lot at 9:25. I ran up the stairs, went to the woman by the checkout register, and said, "My name is Dan Coughlin, and I called a few hours ago about a jacket and a shirt."

A man who was folding clothes four rows over yelled out, "Hey, Dan, we're all ready for you. Here's a cold bottle of water. We didn't think you would have a chance to get anything to drink. Here's your jacket and your shirt. What do you think?"

"I think they look great."

"Try them on and make sure they fit."

I tried them on and they fit perfectly.

He then said, "Now, I did pull out these other two shirts that go with this jacket. What do you think of these?"

I looked at the shirts, I looked back at the salesman, I looked back at the shirts, and I said, "I'll take them."

Why did I spend a thousand dollars that night and why did I think of Nordstrom's?

Three years before that night I was at the Nordstrom's in St. Louis near my house. I had my son, Ben, with me, who was three years old at the time. I went to pick up four pairs of shoes that I had dropped off to be polished. I paid the shoe shine man for the shoes, and then I leaned over to pick up the bag.

He said, "Can I help you?"

I thought he was going to pick up the bag and put it under my arm so I could hold Ben's hand with my other hand. Instead he picked up the bag, left the shoe department unattended, walked out of Nordstrom's, walked out to the parking lot, and put my bag of shoes in the trunk of my car for me so I could focus all of my attention on Ben. Three years later when I was in a jam and couldn't think of anyone else to call the very first company I thought of was Nordstrom's.

Three weeks after he took my shoes out to my car for me, I went back to the Nordstrom's in St. Louis and asked the store manager, "Where do you find all of these friendly people?"

She said, "Oh, it's our interview process."

"Well, what questions do you ask?"

"One of the questions on our questionnaire is, 'Are you a compulsive smiler?' and if the person doesn't break into a smile right away when we ask it, then we probably don't hire that person."

What ideas from that story do you think are important for your work over the next six months?

One idea I want to emphasize is the enormous impact of value and values. Value is anything that increases the chances the other person will achieve what he or she wants to achieve, and values are beliefs that determine behaviors. The shoe shine salesman in St. Louis did not know the shirt salesman in Chicago. They were both just looking for ways to create value and deliver it to a customer. However, it was more than just polishing shoes and selling shirts. They demonstrated really consistent and powerful values. They believed it was okay to go the extra mile and keep the store open and carry my shoes out to my car so I could focus on my son.

It's not just what you provide that matters, but also how you provide it.

When you deliver value to another person and you do so with the appropriate values, the next time that person is in a jam the very first person and the very first organization he or she is going to think of are you and your organization. Your positive impact as a business leader is dependent on both value and values, what you deliver and how you deliver it.

I want you to begin an exercise now that you can come back to several times in the future. I want you to write a list of your values, the beliefs that determine your behaviors. You don't have to think of every conceivable way you can apply those values. I just want you to be aware of your values. Keep that list nearby and read it over regularly and add to it whenever you think of another one of your values.

As you go through your day, ask yourself what you can do to add value to other people in a variety of situations. What is the little extra you can do that would really help the other person? When you do these things, make sure your behaviors always fit within your values. This steady drumbeat of applying value within your values is an effective way for you to steadily make an impact as a business leader.

I also want you to broaden your focus to your entire organization. Any organization that has achieved a sustainable competitive advantage that really matters to customers has done so through a combination of the value it delivers and the values that drive behaviors in the organization. Apple, Wal-Mart, and Disney each have developed a distinctive combination of value and values that have given them a tremendous competitive advantage that really matters to their customers.

Here are a few questions for you to answer to clarify and enhance your organization's sustainable competitive advantage.

1. What value do your customers receive from your organization?

2. What values do people in your organization demonstrate on a regular basis in delivering that value?

3. What competitive advantage can your organization gain and maintain that would really matter to your customers

if the value your organization delivers and the way in which that value is delivered are further honed and strengthened?

I encourage you to include several key people in your organization as you go through these questions in order to arrive at more complete answers. As you influence these individuals to continually think about and refine the organization's value and values, the greater your chances become of crafting a sustainable competitive advantage for your company.

SCHEDULE THINKING AND NON-THINKING TIME

Tom was the Vice-President of Operations of an $800 Million business region. I was working with him as an executive coach. He and I got along very well, and then one day he said to me, "Dan, I have a problem."

I said, "Tom, what is it?"

"My boss thinks I'm not very strategic or creative, and I don't know what to do."

"I have seen this situation many times in the past, and so here is what I suggest."

Tom picked up a pen and said, "This is going to be important. I'm going to want to write this down."

I said, "Tom, I suggest you block out one hour a week to really think. Put it on your calendar and call it thinking time, planning time, or my time, and make it as important as any meeting with any other person. When you get to that hour, I suggest you focus on just one business outcome you want to improve or one business issue you want to resolve. Don't try to brainstorm on five or six things at the same time. Take out a blank sheet of paper and at the top of the sheet of paper turn that business outcome or issue into an open-ended question. Not a yes or no question, but an open-ended question.

"Then for the next 35 minutes answer that question from a variety of perspectives including your perspective, your boss's perspective, your peers' perspective, your employees' perspective, your customers' perspective, and your competitors' perspective. Take the next 10 minutes and look at your list of ideas and combine ideas together to make even better ideas and write them down. At the end of those 45 minutes, select the best idea you came up with and use the last 15 minutes to write out an action plan of how you will move this idea forward. If you will do this for one hour a week, I believe you will make all the other hours in your work week even more effective, and you will be seen as being creative and innovative."

Tom slowly put his pen down and said, "Dan, that is the single dumbest idea I've ever heard. If I go off to La-La Land to think, people are going to make fun of me. You don't understand. People don't pay me to sit around and think. They pay me to get things done."

I said, "Tom, I do understand. People don't pay you to get things done. They pay you to improve results. If you will invest one hour a week in thinking time, you can have a tremendous impact on the results you generate in all the other hours in your work week."

He said, "Fine, I'll try it."

Three weeks went by, and then we spoke again.

Tom said, "I just want you to know I tried your thinking idea, and I can honestly say I wasted three hours."

I said, "Hang in there. It's not going to happen instantly for you."

About two months later he said to me, "I landed on an idea in operations that we've never tried before. Do you think I should try it?"

I said, "Do you think it will have a positive impact on your most important business outcomes?"

"I think it will."

"Do you think it has a high potential to have a really negative impact on your business?"

"I don't think so."

"Well, give it a try."

About four months later we were talking again, and Tom said, "I just want you to know that I now schedule an hour of thinking time every week and everyone on my team schedules an hour a week to think. However, I just have one problem with you. Why didn't you tell me to do this when we first met?"

I didn't have a very good answer so I don't want to make that mistake again. I am encouraging you to block out one hour a week to really think. One hour a week where you get away from your boss, your peers, your employees, your suppliers, your customers, your family, and your dog, and you go to a place where no one knows you. Take out a blank sheet of paper or a computer. Focus on one business issue you want to resolve or one outcome you want to improve. Turn that issue or that outcome into an open-ended question. Answer that question from a variety of perspectives: yours, your boss's, your peers', your employees', your suppliers', your customers', and your competitors'. After 35 minutes look at all of your ideas and start combining them to come up with better ideas. At the end of 45 minutes take your best idea and use the last 15 minutes to put together an action plan. I really believe if you will do this one hour a week you will start to generate even better results.

While we're on the topic of thinking, there is one other topic I want to focus on and that is non-thinking time. One of the worst habits I've seen executives fall into is what I call *The 24 – 7 – 365 Habit*. This is where people feel they need to work 24 hours a day, seven days a week, and 365 days a year in order to survive in the business world. I encourage you to not do that. My experience has been when people work like that they become emotionally exhausted, physically exhausted, and mentally exhausted, and they stop coming up with the kind of ideas that will move their businesses forward.

I encourage you to take breaks from your work. Every morning I suggest you go for a 10-minute walk outside. If it's raining, bring an umbrella. If it's cold, wear a coat. Leave your smart phone on your desk and go out there electronically naked. Every week I suggest you block out at least three consecutive waking hours where you don't touch your email or your texts or your voicemail. Every month I suggest you give yourself at least one full day where you don't touch your work at all. If you will do these things, I believe when you come back to your work you will have greater mental energy and will come up with ideas that can really make a difference in your organization.

Many executives and managers I've met didn't schedule time to really think and never gave themselves a break to mentally rest. They were in constant motion 24/7/365. Unfortunately, for all of their activities and hard work they didn't make much of an impact on the organization's performance or results. They just kept going and going and…

IDENTIFY A LEADER IN YOUR LIFE

Here's a thinking exercise. Think of a person who had a positive influence on your life at any age or under any set of circumstances. Clarify how this person influenced you and what you learned from him or her that you can use in your work today.

Here's an example from my life.

When I was in college I was the third-string, walk-on, non-scholarship goalie on the soccer team all four years. That means when I was a freshman there were two guys ahead of me and when I was a senior there were two guys ahead of me, and it was a different set of two guys. My position on the team was the fourth seat over from the right end of the bench. By my sophomore year if a freshman sat there, the other players would say, "No, no, no. That's where Coughlin sits."

The only times I ever got into a game we were down by four or more goals and my coach, Dennis Grace, would yell out, "Coughlin, come here." I would grab my goalie gloves and run over to him. Then he would say, "I want you to go in there and make a difference." I would run on to the field thinking to myself, "We're down by four goals, there's 10 minutes left in the game, and I'm the goalie. I'm not exactly sure how I'm going to make a difference."

At the end of my four years in college, Coach Grace asked me what I wanted to do for a career. My degree was in mechanical engineering, but I said, "I want to do what you do. I want to be a college soccer coach."

He said, "Well, there actually is a university about 90 miles away that is starting up a brand-new soccer program. Would you like for me to see if I can get you an interview?"

I said, "I would love to get an interview." He got me the interview, and I got the job.

Then Coach Grace said to me, "Would you like to work at the Indiana University Soccer Camp?" IU had four weeks of camp each summer where 600 high school and grade school soccer players would come each week for a total of 2400 campers each summer.

I said, "I would love to work at the IU Soccer Camp." He got me the interview and I got the job.

When I showed up the first day of the camp in 1986, the coaching staff for these kids included a professional soccer player who had played in the World Cup, college head coaches who were in the National Soccer Hall of Fame, high school head coaches who were in the National Soccer Hall of Fame, current college soccer players who were All-American, and me, a guy who sat fourth seat from the right end of the bench and hardly ever got into a game.

I called up Coach Grace and said, "You didn't tell me all these famous coaches were going to be at this camp. How in the world can I coach alongside all of these famous people?"

Then he gave me the single best piece of leadership advice I've ever received. He said, "Dan, just let Dan be Dan. Don't try to be somebody you're not. If you try to act like a big shot, everybody is going to know it and you're going to be a failure. Just let you be you and you will do great."

I encourage you to do the same thing. Just let you be you with your strengths and your passions and your values and you will do great. Don't ever try to be somebody you're not. A trap many executives fall into is they think they have to change who they are or "reinvent" themselves whenever they get a major promotion or a significant change in their responsibilities. The problem occurs when they end up taking themselves away from what made them effective in the first place. You very well may need to address your biggest weakness from getting in your way, but you don't need to reinvent your greatest strength. That's what put you in a position to be promoted.

Now it's your turn.

Think of a leader who impacted your life in a positive way. What did the person do to influence you and what did you learn from this person that you can use in your work today to be a more effective leader? Write out your answers.

Here are two more suggestions. First, the next time you get to your hour of thinking time write down the names of 10 people who had a positive influence on your life. Next to each name write down one or two lessons you learned from this person on how to be an effective leader. That list of ideas will serve as a great leadership toolkit for you to draw on many times in the future. Second, send a thank you note with some small gift to each of these individuals letting him or her know what a great influence he or she had on your life. You might reach back to people you haven't talked to for decades. They deserve to know the impact they made on you.

THE FOUR CRITICAL LEADERSHIP QUESTIONS

Since I graduated from college in 1985, the topic I have studied the most by far is leadership. I've read more than 500 books, most of which had something to do with leadership. I coached or taught more than 1,200 college and high school students before I started my own leadership consulting firm in 1998. Since then I have served as an executive coach for more than 180 executives and have provided more than 2,100 executive coaching sessions. I have also worked with over 200 organizations and have invested more than 3,000 hours on-site observing and advising executives in the regular flow of their workday.

From all of this research on leadership a few things have really stood out for me.

First, as I mentioned earlier, leadership means influencing how people think so they make decisions that improve results in a sustainable way. Second, leaders take time to think. They don't rush into action immediately. They consider what to do before they do it. Third, every effective leader I've either worked with or observed has taken the time to step back and answer what I call *The Four Critical Leadership Questions*. Most of the time they didn't do this in a step-by-step process like I'm going to guide you through, but they did take time to figure out their answers. Here are the four questions:

Question #1: What outcome for your organization do you want to improve the most and why did you select that outcome?

Prioritization is the first act of leadership. The most common mistake among newly promoted managers is they try to impact too many outcomes simultaneously, and consequently they dilute their impact on all of them and end up with mediocre results at best. It is a courageous act of leadership to clarify a specific desired outcome as being the most important one because it leaves you open to criticism for not having chosen something else. Do it anyway. Be crystal clear about the most important desired outcome.

Question #2: Who do you need to influence in order to improve that outcome and why did you select these people?

Who are the key individuals or key groups of individuals that will have the greatest impact, positively or negatively, on the desired outcome? Until you know who you are trying to influence you can waste an enormous amount of time. Write down the names of the individuals or groups you are going to focus on.

Question #3: How do you want these people to think so they make decisions that improve this outcome in a sustainable way?

What few steps do you want them to consider thinking through or what key ideas do you want them to keep in mind before they make a decision regarding the outcome you want to improve? If you get them focused on too many things, you will dilute your impact as a leader. You can't be present in every situation with every one of these individuals to solve every problem. However, your influence can be present because you have given them steps to consider or ideas to remember.

Notice the third question doesn't say, "What do you need to tell them to do?" Telling employees what to do is micromanaging. At best, you might improve short-term results through micromanaging, but you may very well end up with some serious problems. You might get employees who can't think for themselves, a lack of a leadership pipeline, and good people who leave to go where they are encouraged to think for themselves. Leadership is not about micromanaging. It is about influencing how people think.

Question #4: What will you do and say to influence how these people think?

This is the art of leadership. When confronted with a leadership situation, I encourage you to think through what you are specifically going to do and say to influence how other people think. If you always rely on what you have done in the past or what comes naturally for you, you might end up reducing your effectiveness as a leader.

WAYS TO INFLUENCE HOW OTHER PEOPLE THINK

Here are 15 ways to influence how other people think. As you read through these different leadership approaches, I encourage you to think of either a famous person or someone you know personally who has demonstrated this approach. This will help you bring each approach to life and make it more of a tangible option for you.

The Example – this person's behaviors model the desired behavior.

For our 10th wedding anniversary my wife, Barb, and I wanted to do something really, really different. We wanted to get away from our kids. I mean that in a positive way. We positively wanted to get away from our kids. Three months before our anniversary I came downstairs to the kitchen and Barb was sitting at the kitchen table flipping through a glossy vacation catalog.

She looked up and said, "Dan, sit here. Look at these two pictures and tell me which one you like better."

I took the catalog and looked at the two pictures and pointed to the one on the right. "I like this one better."

She said, "Okay."

Three months later I was standing under a thatched roof with water up to my waist at a swim-up bar in Mexico drinking a foo-foo drink and watching Barb do water aerobics. I was thinking to myself, "This is paradise. For the next five days I am not going to read any books, I'm not going to write any books, and I'm not looking for any ideas on how to accelerate results. I am just going to stand at this swim-up bar and enjoy my foo-foo drinks."

Then it happened.

I noticed Barb was doing water aerobics. She likes to walk and she likes to play tennis, but she hates aerobics, and yet there she was with about 15 other women pumping her arms and legs. I couldn't figure out what was going on until I looked a little farther over and saw a tall, dark, and handsome man. His name was Cesar, and he was the teacher of the aerobics class. Whatever he did these 15 women did.

The next day we were playing water volleyball. There were a bunch of little kids, some young adults, and some older adults playing, and we were all laughing. I looked behind me and saw that with a whistle around his neck the coach was Cesar.

The next day after dinner everyone was up and dancing with their partner, and we were all having a great time. I looked up at the stage and saw that dressed in a tuxedo the emcee was Cesar.

It hit me that the reason we were all having so much fun is because he was having so much fun. Even the other employees seemed to light up even more when Cesar was around.

The next day, after Barb got her picture taken with Cesar, I interviewed him.

I said, "Cesar, how long have you worked at this resort?"

He said, "Two years."

"How many weeks of vacation do you get every year?"

"Two weeks."

"How many days a week to you work here?

"Five days."

This meant by the time we got to Mexico Cesar had already been on the job for 500 days, but he had the enthusiasm of someone who was on the job for the very first time.

I said, "Cesar, how do you maintain your enthusiasm every single day?"

He looked at me and paused. Then he said, "Well, when people come to my resort they want to have a great time, and I'm going to do everything I can to make sure that happens."

Cesar had a purpose and that purpose drove his enthusiasm. By his example, he influenced guests and employees to have more fun each day.

Is there a way you can be The Example for your employees? Is there some behavior you want people in your organization to consistently display, and can you influence them through your example?

The Calm Observer – this person stays calm in the midst of chaotic conversations and then offers a perspective to the group.

Lou was one of the most effective executives I ever had the chance to work with. (By the way, all of the names of my clients have been changed from the person's real name, and sometimes I've changed the person's gender as well. I don't want you to fall into any kind of gender stereotypes so

I won't be announcing when I've changed the gender.) He was The Calm Observer. I saw him in action at more than two dozen meetings where he was the person in charge of the group. While someone else facilitated, Lou would take a seat somewhere within the group. He would listen attentively for the first 30 minutes or so and take notes. Then he would raise his hand to get in the queue to share his comments.

When his turn came up he would start off by quoting what other people had said earlier in the meeting. By doing this, he helped people to realize he was really listening to them, and in turn they now really listened to what he had to say. Then he would calmly provide his insights and suggestions. This approach allowed for a more collaborative discussion to unfold. Over a period of weeks and months I watched as ideas came to fruition and steadily improved business results. By staying calm he was able to reduce the amount of time and energy that was wasted on drama and negative emotions.

His calmness allowed him to retain a healthy detachment from the emotional chaos and he was able to rationally look at the business both in terms of day-to-day performance and overall systems in the business and its approach to the marketplace. Then he guided rational discussions to figure out what needed to be done next.

The Teacher – this person breaks down the idea and explains it very clearly.

Is there a complicated concept or process that is keeping people in your organization from being as effective as they can be? Can you break that concept down into much smaller parts and explain each of those parts to people in your organization, and then show how all of the parts fit together?

The Listener – this person listens while the other person shares an idea.

Caryn was the Regional Vice-President of a $900 Million business region, and she was a phenomenal listener. I watched as Caryn interacted with people in one-on-one conversations, in meetings of eight people, and in conferences of 200 people, and she always listened amazingly well. If someone brought up an idea, she would listen with total focus on the person. That helped the person feel empowered to keep explaining his or her idea in more depth. In doing so, the idea became richer and stronger and more detailed. Many times these ideas that started off by someone making a point ended up being realities that improved results. It all started because Caryn really listened.

The Storyteller – this person tells a down-to-earth story that conveys a powerful point.

Is there some experience you've had recently where you gained an insight into a particular behavior that you want to see more of in your organization? Can you tell the story to a group of your employees and then end the story by emphasizing a particular point? This was one of Abraham Lincoln's and Mark Twain's greatest strengths. Their stories and the points they were emphasizing have lived on for more than a hundred years after they each died. A well-crafted story with a powerful point can really influence how other people think.

The Facilitator – this person asks questions and gets multiple people involved in sharing their insights.

Many times when I worked with someone as an executive coach he or she called me up three months into our relationship and said, "Dan, I learned something today."

I said, "What is it?"

"I learned I don't have to have all the answers."

"That's good because you don't have to have all the answers."

By taking an important issue in your business and turning it into an open-ended question, you can both guide the conversation and gather meaningful insights from a variety of people. One of the most effective meetings I've ever attended was a McDonald's meeting where four restaurant managers sat on bar stools at the front of a room with about 30 McDonald's owner/operators and corporate executives in the audience. The regional vice-president facilitated a conversation between the restaurant managers and the audience members on a variety of topics. In this way, the owners and the executives were able to see the business issues in new ways that influenced how they thought about future initiatives.

The Researcher - this person studies a topic with great depth and shares the findings.

Jason Jennings has written several best-selling business books where he selected a single topic and then spent years researching that topic and then honed his findings down to a few relevant insights for readers. Is there a topic in your organization or your industry that you can study and research in great depth, and then come back to the people in your organization and share your findings? In doing so, you may very well affect how people in your organization think about that topic in the future.

The Coach – this person engages the other person in a conversation through meaningful questions and offers advice based on watching his or her performance.

In an athletic event, the coach stands on the sideline and observes the players. He or she watches what each player does that is effective and ineffective. When a player comes off the field the coach shares those observations and discusses them with the person.

You can do the same in your business. Observe an employee while he or she is in action. Don't interrupt the person or intervene to help. Just watch. Then when the activity is over share what you observed and engage the other person in a private conversation about what just happened. You might say, "I noticed every time Colleen spoke you listened, but every time Suzanne spoke you interrupted her. Why is that?" By basing your input on observed behaviors rather than on general statements, you can have a greater impact on the individual.

The Orchestrator – this person thinks through the sequence of activities and conversations that need to occur in order to improve a result.

Through discussions with executives in a wide variety of corporations I've learned that it is not enough to know what to do and who to meet with in order to improve a result or gain support for a new project. You have to think through the order of who to talk to first, second, and third, and which activity needs to be accomplished first, second, and third. If you just move into action without orchestrating the sequence of people and events, then you may very well never gain any support or momentum for the project.

The Visionary – this person explains clearly what success will look like when it is achieved.

This was Walt Disney's particular strength. In the making of the film, *Snow White*, he acted out the parts of Snow White, the evil queen, and the seven dwarfs so the animators could see what the final version was supposed to look like.

Can you explain to your employees what success will look like two years from now for your organization or your part of the organization? Can you add in detailed descriptions and explain it with enthusiasm so the picture of success becomes crystal clear for everyone? In doing so, you will help people see how their efforts today are moving toward making that vision a reality.

The Encourager – this person finds opportunities to encourage other people to do their best work.

My dad died on March 18, 2009. It was the day after St. Patrick's Day. My dad was a great big Irishman and St. Patrick's Day was his favorite day of the year so he hung in there for one more day. One of the things I loved the most about my dad was his encouragement.

Dad would watch another person in action. Then after the activity was over he would call the other person over to him, and he would say, "I just want you to know that I'm really, really proud of you for the way you handled that situation." Then he would point out specific things that had happened so the other person knew he really was being sincere.

When you watch people in your organization at work and you see someone do something that really demonstrates an important behavior, go up to them and say, "I am really proud of you for the way you handled that difficult situation with a customer. (Or whatever it was.) I noticed how you calmly listened and then delivered real help to that person. Thank you very much."

The Promoter – this person explains clearly and passionately why something is really special and worthwhile.

I've known people who worked for a company for over 35 years and never said a bad thing about the organization. When they interacted with family members and friends and people in their neighborhood, they always spoke positively about the business. This had a very real way of influencing how other people thought about the organization.

Are you a promoter of your organization or do you tear it down when you are on your home turf? The way you view your company will impact the way you interact with your co-workers.

The Advocate – this person throws his or her support behind a specific person, group, or cause.

What are you an advocate for? What do you put your time, energy, and money behind? What you advocate for says a lot about your values, and this can significantly influence how other people think. If you are an advocate for mentoring new employees and you demonstrate that by investing your time and energy into this activity, you can influence how other people think about mentoring.

The Challenger – this person gives a meaningful challenge to an individual or a group of people that causes them to stretch beyond what they are used to doing.

After Jimmy Carter graduated from the U.S. Naval Academy in the 1940s, he applied for a position at the Naval Nuclear Program with Admiral Hyman Rickover. Admiral Rickover asked Carter how he did at the Naval Academy.

Carter swelled with pride and said, "I graduated 59th out of a class of 820."

Rickover asked, "Did you do your best?"

Carter wanted to say yes, but then he paused and thought about the question. He said, "No sir, I didn't do my best."

Rickover asked, "Why not the best?"

Jimmy Carter went on to say in his book, *Why Not The Best?* that this question, "Why not the best?" was the key challenge that spurred him on throughout his career. Eventually this challenge carried him to be the president of the United States and a Nobel Peace Prize winner.

Is there a challenge you can provide to your team members individually or collectively that might cause them to stretch beyond where they are today?

The Personal Touch – this person leverages the power of the handwritten note.

My mom is and always has been a great leader. When I was 12 years old and I received a check for $10 from my Aunt Helen, Mom said, "Now, Danny, (for the record my mom is the only one who is allowed to call me Danny) you need to write a thank you letter to your Aunt Helen." When I was a senior in college and I received a scholarship to go to college, Mom said, "Danny, you need to write a thank you letter to each of the members of that committee." When I was 22 years old and I got my first job, Mom said, "Danny, you need to write a thank you letter to your new boss." When I was 50 years old and my high school teacher's father died, Mom said, "Danny, I saw that Mr. Becvar's father died. You need to write a thank you letter to Mr. Becvar for all that he did for you."

I've been sending handwritten letters for over 40 years, and they are more important now than ever before. In a world of texts, emails, twitters, voice mail, and blogs, a handwritten letter can have an extraordinary impact on another person. I encourage you to write at least one handwritten letter every week to an employee or a customer or a supplier. A handwritten letter says you took the time to really think about another person and to reach out in a personal way to strengthen the relationship.

THE FOUR CRITICAL LEADERSHIP QUESTIONS (APPLIED)

Here are the four questions again. I encourage you to carve out thirty minutes over the next 48 hours to answer these questions one at a time.

1. What outcome for my organization do I want to improve the most and why did I select that outcome?

2. Who do I need to influence in order to improve that outcome?

3. How do I want these people to think so they make decisions that improve this outcome in a sustainable way?

4. What will I do to influence how they think?

By taking the time to answer these questions, I believe you will move into your next leadership moment with a clearer plan on how to make a significant difference in that situation. One recommendation I have for you is don't try to use all 15 leadership approaches, but also don't try to rely on just one. I suggest you consider four or five different approaches that you can use in different situations.

AVOID DISASTROUS LEADERSHIP APPROACHES

While there are many ways to be an effective leader, there are also a variety of ways to be a disastrous leader. A disastrous leadership style is an approach that can't sustain its impact over the long term primarily because it's all about what's good for the person and not about what's good for the organization. Here are 10 disastrous leadership approaches that I have seen business executives and managers demonstrate.

The Chameleon – this person changes his or her opinions depending on who is in the room or who is on the conference call.

A chameleon is a lizard. It's a lizard that changes its color in order to match its surroundings. Being a chameleon in the forest is a good thing because it allows the lizard to stay alive. Being a chameleon in an organization is a bad thing because no one knows what the person stands for.

Bob had five different bosses over a period of four years. I worked directly and indirectly with Bob for those four years. Three of his bosses were promoted, one got fired, and then he had his fifth boss.

Whenever I was alone with Bob he would say, "What do I need to do to get promoted?"

I would say, "Provide great leadership, get great results, and you will get promoted."

Whenever he was alone with his boss, he would ask what he needed to do to get promoted and they told him the same thing I was telling him. The reason I know that is because his bosses would tell me what had happened.

Bob had a different strategy. He thought the key to getting promoted was to find out what was important to the boss of the moment and then say things that supported what the boss wanted. He would even use the same verbiage as the boss. When one boss was all about speed of delivery, Bob would say in front of his colleagues, "As you all know, I've always believed speed is the most important thing." When the next boss wanted great customer service, Bob said, "As you all know, I've always said the most important thing we can do every day is to meet the needs of our customers no matter how long it takes."

Bob's fellow employees would stop me in the hallway and say, "Who is this guy? Six months ago he said something totally different than what he said today. I don't get it."

Over the next 10 years Bob never did get promoted. He finally took a lateral move to a different part of the company. Bob worked hard and he did deliver very good results, but the reason he never got promoted is because no one knew what he stood for. He had no leadership platform that people could trust. Inconsistency as a leader causes people to lose trust in you because they don't know what you are going to stand for tomorrow.

The Polite Dictator – this person smiles, asks for input, ignores others, and makes all the decisions.

Ken was the new division president of a $5 Billion division in a Fortune 200 company. He was speaking in front of 500 people at a big regional meeting. I was in the room because I was coaching some of the other executives at the meeting.

Ken said to the audience, "For us to be as good as we can be I need your best thinking on our newest initiative. I want you to really think about what would be the best way to roll this out and then email me your best ideas. I will read every idea and consider it as we move toward making our final decision. Together we can make magic happen." When he walked off the stage he received a standing ovation.

Later that day I saw Ken in the restroom, and I said, "Ken, you don't know me, but I wanted you to know I thought it was really tremendous when you asked the audience for their best ideas to help you with your decision."

He said, "Oh, I've already made my decision on what we're going to do."

"Well then why did you ask them to email you their best ideas?"

"It's a trick I learned years ago. It's a way of getting them all excited. They'll forget I even asked for it by the end of the day."

A few years later Ken was fired. He had the worst employee engagement scores of any division president and his customer retention was the lowest of any division in the company. The Polite Dictator says what is needed to please people for the moment, but doesn't realize that people quickly stop trusting him or her.

The Dutiful Employee – this person always waits to be told what to do and refuses to think for himself or herself.

At first this employee is highly valued because the boss will give him or her a variety of important projects and tasks to accomplish and this person will come through every time. The problem occurs when the boss realizes that this person always waits to be told what to do. He or she never steps forward with an idea on how to improve the business or how to do something in a better way. At this point the boss realizes that he or she has to always think for The Dutiful Employee and sees that this person can never be promoted into a leadership position in the organization.

The Perennial Student – this person focuses only on learning more without applying the insights.

The key to improving performance is not accumulating knowledge. The key is to learn, tweak, and apply. Learning from other people is important. Try to do it every day. Then ask yourself what you can adjust or add to what you have learned that will make it even more effective for your situation. Then apply that learning. The Perennial Student wants to read every book and attend every seminar and sign up to be mentored by every senior executive in the company, but then he or she doesn't want to apply that knowledge. That's a huge waste of an opportunity for the person and for the company.

The Superhero – this person keeps working longer hours in an attempt to continually improve results.

This person thinks if his or her predecessor got pretty good results working 40 hours a week than he or she will produce amazing results by working 80 hours a week. At first people admire this person's superhuman effort and the results do improve for awhile. The problem sets in when this person thinks that just putting in longer hours is the key to success. It's not the number of hours that produces better results, but the number of quality hours. The other problem occurs when this person thinks he or she is a superhero who will never tire out. Eventually burnout sets in and this person becomes very ineffective.

The Coattail Rider – this person has a great relationship with a key executive or customer and leverages the relationship in every situation.

This is the son or daughter of the owner or a great friend of the general manager who makes it very clear to everyone in the organization that the key to success is the relationship with the boss rather than the results that are achieved. While this person has a big title, other people realize that if they want to get anything done they are going to have to work around this person. The Coattail Rider becomes one of the major obstacles for people and is ultimately rendered pointless as a leader of any significance.

Not every relative or friend of the boss is a Coattail Rider. Many are extraordinary performers and deserve their position. Just be careful that you never allow your relationship with your boss to be the primary driver of future promotions.

The I'll-get-the-results-no-matter-what-it-takes Approach - this person tosses out ethics on the road to hitting a number.

Bernard Madoff. Bernie Ebbers. Jeff Skilling. The names have almost slipped away from people's memories, yet they all cheated big time and robbed their companies and society of tens of millions of dollars. If you can't operate with integrity, you cannot be a great business leader. It really is that simple and straightforward.

The Arrogant Leader - the arrogant leader thinks he or she has all the answers and has nothing left to learn.

I'm thinking about writing another book someday called, *The Arrogant Executive: how to ruin a business in five minutes or less.* The Arrogant Leader works in the ultimate silo, one in which no one else's ideas ever penetrate his or her brain. Soon employees stop trying to offer ideas and eventually they stop pouring their passion and talent toward supporting this person.

The I've-arrived Approach - this person has had great success in the past as a leader and feels that his or her reputation alone will generate great results.

While this person still has the capacity to add value in the current situation, he or she will constantly think about the past glories and talk about how his or her old employees are better than the current ones. Rather than focusing on improving the current team members, this person constantly complains that these people aren't any good compared to the stars of the past. This grates on employees until they completely stop listening to this person, and results get worse and worse.

The Constant Intervener - this person is knowledgeable and has real value to offer, but overwhelms people by constantly offering advice and correcting them in every situation.

Giving advice to another person can be really helpful in improving a situation. However, if the advice becomes more like machine gun fire, then it becomes overwhelmingly ineffective. Employees get sick to death of being given advice every time they turn around, and yet The Constant Intervener keeps stepping into every project and every situation to offer more suggestions. You have to pick your moments to offer advice or other people will eventually tune you out even if you're the CEO. It's human nature to say, "Enough is enough. Either trust me or fire me." More on this situation in a moment.

In summary, while there is definitely more than one way to be an effective leader, there is also a wide range of ways to be ineffective. The common denominators of ineffective leaders are they always put themselves ahead of the good of the organization and they are inconsistent in what they stand for to the point other people cannot trust them.

TWO CRITICAL THINGS TO KNOW ABOUT YOURSELF

Two factors above all others will determine your ability to become a more effective business leader. They are your greatest strength and your greatest weakness.

I don't want you to spend too much time worrying about all of your characteristics. Just focus on answering this question: what is your greatest strength and what is your greatest weakness? At this point in your life your greatest strength will probably remain your greatest strength and your greatest weakness will, unfortunately, remain your greatest weakness. Despite all of the talk about how much people change during their career, I believe at their core they stay very much the same.

It's going to take some effort on your part to find the answer to this question. That's okay because it's going to be worth it. Make a list of 20 people who know you well. Ask them to answer this question about you: in your opinion, what is my greatest strength and what is my greatest weakness? Don't make it complicated for them and don't get defensive. Just ask them to consider the question for awhile and to get back to you whenever they are ready. See if you can find any common themes in their answers. Then spend some time reflecting about yourself as though you were having an out-of-body experience. As you think back over your lifetime what would you say has become your greatest strength and your greatest weakness?

The reasons why these are so important to uncover are because I want you to actively spend the vast majority of your time using your greatest strength and I want you to consciously avoid letting your greatest weakness get in the way of your success. Too often busy people let their time get used up while barely ever using their greatest strength. Also, many people I've observed could have been much more successful, but they let their greatest weakness ruin their performance over and over again. I'll give you a few examples of what I mean from people I have worked with as an executive coach.

Lessons on Using Strengths and Addressing Weaknesses

Larry was a senior-level operations executive in a massive corporation by the time I met him. His great strength was his ability to organize. Given any responsibility, he could organize the people involved and the tasks to be completed and deliver consistently good results. He told me when he was in high school the principal often asked him to organize school events because of his ability to figure out what needed to be done and how to organize groups of students to accomplish everything on time. He had used this strength to carve out a very successful career.

His weakness was he didn't come up with breakthrough ideas on how to move the business forward. He was seen as an "operations guy," but not as a creative or innovative executive. He turned this situation around by making creativity and innovation into a process that he could organize. In other words, he applied his greatest strength to his greatest weakness.

On a weekly basis he sat down with a legal pad and went through a series of questions: what do our customers need, what are we currently doing that we can do better for them to help them achieve what they need, how can we take something our competitors are doing and do it better than them for our customers, and what else can we do for our customers that we are not currently doing? After he answered these questions by himself, he got other people involved in answering them. Then he took the best answers and began to organize them into projects. Over the course of the next decade Larry was promoted five times and was put in charge of one of the most innovative nation-wide projects in the company's history.

Is there a way you can apply your greatest strength toward your greatest weakness and make your impact on the business even stronger?

At the time I met her Cathy was a senior-level operations person who was being groomed to take over an $800 Million business region. Cathy's greatest strength was her inspirational public speaking skills. She had been an athlete in college, and she had a vibrancy and charisma in front of a group that drew rave reviews from audience members. She was very attractive, stayed in great physical shape, and prepared her remarks until they were chiseled. She had a movie star quality that really came across powerfully from the stage.

Her weakness was she was almost too perfect and some people had a very hard time relating to her as a real person. They didn't feel she was very genuine or down-to-earth in her remarks. To break through this weakness she crafted handwritten letters to many of the audience members encouraging them to keep doing their best work. She would mail as many as 50 handwritten letters in a week.

These letters began to change her image as being too perfect. They became her way of building personal connections with people in her business. She also started telling self-deprecating humorous stories. This also helped the audience members to feel she was just like them and they could accomplish what she had accomplished. One time she talked about missing an easy layup in the last minute of a state championship basketball game. Then she turned to the audience and said, "I've never forgotten the importance of being prepared for life's biggest moments. Don't make the mistake I made. Focus on the fundamentals." I can still picture how the audience was riveted on her story and the impact that story had on their performance over the next 60 days. Customer service scores went up dramatically after that conference.

Is there an action you could take to reduce the impact of your greatest weakness?

In many ways, Mary was more talented than Larry or Cathy. She was very bright, very hard-working, and very knowledgeable about the business she was running. I'm confident she knew more about every part of the business than any other person among the 300 people working there.

Her weakness was her competitiveness. Not only did she want her business to compete successfully in the marketplace, which was a good thing, but she also wanted to compete with every manager in the business in every discussion. She acted as though she had to win every conversation and prove that she was right and they were wrong.

In a day-long meeting, I watched as she interrupted and corrected her management team members more than 150 times as they were making presentations. When I reminded her a week later that her compulsive competitiveness was driving her team members crazy, which is what they had told me when I interviewed them at the beginning of our executive coaching relationship, she started to "compete" with me. She argued that she was highly engaged in the meeting, which was true and that part was healthy, and that she was just trying to help people to understand the business better, which unfortunately didn't work out because they kept tuning her out.

After our phone call she told members of her staff that she had proved me "wrong" and that clearly she knew more than me about how to run the business. The only problem was I wasn't competing with her. Of course she knew more than me about her business. I was just suggesting that she consider listening for longer periods of time and not interrupt people in the middle of a sentence every 45 seconds for an entire day.

In the end, Mary was not nearly as effective as a business leader as she could have been because she refused to make any adjustments regarding her greatest weakness. She continued to dominate people in order to "win" conversations and "prove" she was the smartest person in the room on every business topic. Her ability to influence how her managers thought about the business was greatly diminished because she wouldn't stop competing with them and they wanted to stay as far away from her as they could.

Lesson: extremely good traits do not outweigh extremely bad traits. You do have to address your greatest weakness.

Are you letting your greatest weakness keep you from achieving what you are capable of achieving as a business leader?

Be honest with yourself. You don't have to prove me or anyone else wrong about your weakness.

If your greatest weakness is continually getting in your way, what can you do to address it?

This is a chapter on leadership. The starting point of leadership effectiveness is to know your greatest strength and your greatest weakness. Then spend most of your working day applying your greatest strength and make sure your greatest weakness is being addressed in a way that keeps it from getting in your way.

OPERATE AT THE INTERSECTION OF GREAT PERFORMANCES FOR A VERY LONG TIME

Before we move on to a different topic, I want to add a little more depth to the topic of your greatest strengths. In studying great performers I have noticed the same pattern occurs over and over. For example, if you read *Steve Jobs* by Walter Isaacson, *Walt Disney* by Neal Gabler, *Mockingbird* by Charles Shields, which is the biography of Harper Lee, the novelist who wrote *To Kill a Mockingbird*, and Alice Schroeder's *The Snowball*, which is a biography of Warren Buffett, I believe you will see the same pattern. These extraordinary performers, and others like them, spent the vast majority of their time applying their greatest strengths and their greatest passions toward a meaningful objective, and the whole time they did it while operating within their own values, their beliefs about how they should do their work.

I encourage you to answer these questions.

1. What is your greatest strength and what is your greatest passion?

2. What are your values when it comes to work? In other words, what beliefs do you have about how you should do your work?

3. What is the most important outcome you want to improve for your organization?

4. How can you use your greatest strength and your greatest passion to improve that outcome while still operating within your own values?

These are going to require a little time on your part to answer right now, and then probably a lot more time as you continue to think about those questions down the road. If you really want to improve your impact as a business leader over the long term, spend most of your day using your greatest strength and your greatest passion toward improving your most important business outcome while still operating within your own values. Then do that over and over again for a very, very, very long time.

Dr. Anders Ericsson is a professor and researcher at Florida State University, and one of the writers I respect the most on great performers. His work has influenced many of the most popular books on great performers including *Outliers* by Malcolm Gladwell, *Talent is Overrated* by Geoffrey Colvin, *Bounce* by Matthew Syed, and *The Genius In All of Us* by David Shenk.

Anders Ericsson is practically a national treasure, and yet very few people know of him because his work focuses on learning about expert performance rather than on promoting Anders Ericsson. He has spent virtually his entire career studying how extraordinary performers reach their pinnacles of success. He has studied memory experts, pianists, military leaders, medical doctors, and a wide range of other great performers. Two of Dr. Ericsson's most famous insights are called "deliberate practice" and "The 10,000-hour Rule." He found the greatest performers practiced their particular activity in very specific ways for a period of roughly 10,000 hours before they reached a level of what he called "expert performance."

Think about that for a moment. If you work 40 hours a week for 50 weeks a year, that's 2,000 hours. It would take you five solid years of applying your greatest strength and your greatest passion toward improving specific business outcomes while always being true to your values before you would reach a level of expert performance. Since it's virtually impossible to do that every hour of every working day, it's more likely it will take you 10 years or more to reach this level. Of course, once you reach it you will need to continue operating at that level in order to make the greatest impact you are capable of making.

This is why I believe you need to maintain a laser-like focus on continually applying your greatest strength and greatest passion throughout the work day. Don't let your time be eaten up on trivial stuff like whining about where your desk is or getting caught up in the soap operas at work.

KNOW THE IMPORTANCE OF YOUR BELIEF SYSTEM

Sports psychologist and professional counselor Tom Michler said at a meeting I attended, "One of the key points we try to get across to athletes is they cannot consistently outperform their own belief system. They will never consistently achieve a result they don't believe they are capable of achieving. Of course, it takes hard work and commitment and skill and talent, but it also takes belief within the individual."

That is such an insightful statement. You may not achieve everything you believe you can achieve, but you are very unlikely to consistently achieve more than you think you can achieve. Psychological factors definitely play an important role in your ability to make an impact as a business leader, and I'm going to touch on that concept a bit right now.

Self-confidence in a business sense is the degree to which you believe you are going to be successful in guiding your organization to greater success in the future. Your level of self-confidence as an executive will provide the upper parameter to which you will be able to consistently achieve. Even though you are responsible for a significant portion, if not all, of your business, please don't underestimate the importance of your internal beliefs. This topic is an important factor in you helping to guide your organization to better sustainable results.

There are two ways that I know of for strengthening self-confidence. The first is to review your past successes, and the second is to preview your future successes.

Take some time very soon to review one of your past successes. Try to clear out everything else you're thinking about and just relive that success story. Relive it as though it just happened. Here are five questions to answer in order to relive that experience.

1. What was the goal you were trying to achieve?

2. What were the obstacles you faced?

3. How did you persevere through those challenges?

4. What did it feel like for you when you achieved the goal?

5. What lessons from that experience can you apply in your current business situation to help you achieve what you want for your organization?

If all you do is read what I just wrote, you aren't going to get much out of it. Actually you'll get less than zero because you did invest some time in reading it. That time and the opportunity to improve will be lost if you don't do something with these questions. I encourage you to close this book and really focus on this real-life success story from your past. If you do, I'll bet you'll remember certain sounds, smells, feelings, and tiny details from the story you haven't thought about for years. Just go through those five questions and answer them one at a time.

Your story might be about a team you tried out for as a kid and you didn't know if you could make it or not, but then your confidence grew and you ended up being a starter, or perhaps you could recall your first job out of college and how you weren't sure if you could handle the pressure and you ended up getting promoted.

By investing five minutes in this exercise, you will see you've already been down this road before where you wanted to achieve something that had a lot of obstacles to overcome, you persevered, made adjustments, believed in yourself, and finally achieved the objective. Now apply that same sense of confidence and the lessons you drew out of this past success story to the challenges you are facing at work today. Make a deliberate connection between your past success story and your current work situation.

To preview a future success story, answer these three questions.

1. What do you want to achieve?

2. Why do you want to achieve it?

3. Why do you believe you are going to achieve it?

This is another simple exercise for increasing your belief, which is the upper boundary of your capacity for consistently achieving great results, but it has no value if you just read it and don't apply it. I'm going to go through these three questions one more time, and as I do so I hope you will write down your answers.

What do you want to achieve? What is the most important outcome in your organization that you want to improve in the next six months? What level of improvement do you want to accomplish? Be as clear and as specific as you can. Write it down.

Why do you want to achieve this level of improvement? What are all the benefits you can think of if you accomplish this? What are the benefits for you as an individual, your family, your department, your organization, your suppliers, your customers, and your shareholders? Write down every benefit you can think of. When you've got all your reasons written down, then push yourself for two more minutes to add to your list.

Why do you believe you will achieve what you are setting out to achieve? What are all the reasons why you believe this is going to become a reality? What do you bring to the party? What do your employees bring? What do other departments bring? What do other executives bring? What do your suppliers bring? Write down every single reason why you believe your organization will achieve this desired improvement. When you're all done, go back and challenge yourself to add even more reasons as to why you believe it's going to happen.

If you invest eight minutes in answering these questions, I think you will look down at your paper and feel how much more realistic achieving this desired reality is for you. Then read your answers over again and again in the months to come. You probably won't achieve something consistently if you don't believe it will happen. You probably won't achieve something consistently just because you believe it will happen. You might very well achieve something consistently if you believe it will happen AND you work toward making it happen.

BEWARE OF THE TRAPS OF IRRATIONAL OPTIMISM AND IRRATIONAL PESSIMISM

Strengthening your belief about what you can achieve is very important. However, be careful not to fall into the trap of becoming too emotionally connected to your results. This is a pattern I have noticed in my work with business executives since 1998. I call this *The Psychology of Results*. Here is how the pattern works.

When a person achieves a result that is better than was expected, he or she becomes pretty excited. When it happens a second time where the actual result is better than the expected result, the person becomes really excited. When it happens a third time, the person becomes irrationally optimistic and thinks the good times are going to last forever and results are just going to get better and better and better all the time. On the other hand, when a person achieves a result that is less than what he or she expected, the person gets a little bummed out. When it happens two times in a row, the person gets really bummed out. When it happens three times in a row where the actual result is less than the expected result, the person becomes flat out irrationally pessimistic and thinks the bad times are going to stick around forever and things are just going to get worse and worse.

In both situations notice the person has subconsciously removed himself or herself from the process of improving the future. This person acts as though the future is permanently great or permanently terrible and there is nothing that can be done about it.

I encourage you to avoid this emotional roller coaster. Be passionate in pursuing results, but stay logical in analyzing results. While emotions can drive remarkable performances, they can also take us away from seeing obvious things that will solve our problems.

When my daughter, Sarah, was eight years old, she invited five other girls over for a sleepover. After we made pizzas and played games, we finally got the girls down to sleep in sleeping bags around 11 PM on our living room floor. About 25 minutes later Sarah came running upstairs to our bedroom. She said, "Mom, Dad, we hear keys rattling downstairs and we're not sure where the noise is coming from."

Barb and I ran downstairs. We checked the kitchen and the basement and all around the house. Then we finally realized that the noise was the zippers on the sleeping bags. The more nervous the girls became, the louder the zippers got, and the louder the zippers got, the more nervous the girls became. We had to stay logical in order to solve the problem.

This is true for business leaders as well. If you get caught up in being overly optimistic or pessimistic by looking at your results, then you might keep yourself from identifying and solving the underlying issues that can improve results in the future.

The Raising Your Performance Bar Process

Steve was a results driven executive, and the reason I know that is because the very first time I met him he said, "I'm a results driven executive."

I said, "Well, that's good because the job of an executive is to improve results in a sustainable way."

Over the next 30 minutes Steve told me four more times he was a results driven executive so I finally asked him what he meant by it.

He said, "At the beginning of every quarter we set a goal. At the end of the quarter, if we achieve or exceed the goal, we have a celebration. If we don't hit the goal, I come down pretty hard on people. Sometimes I fire people just to get the point across that we have to hit our goals."

I said, "How much money are you leaving on the table using that approach?"

He said, "I'm not leaving any money on the table. What are you talking about?"

I looked at him for a few seconds, and then I said, "Steve, how much time and energy are your employees wasting while they are worrying about achieving the goal that they could be using to actually improve their results?"

He said, "I have heard it's pretty nerve-racking to work for me, but, hey, that's business."

I said, "All you're doing is answering the first question, but there are three more questions to answer."

He said, "What are you talking about?"

I said, "All you're answering is, 'What was our goal three months ago and what have we achieved today?' But there are three more questions for everyone to consider. The first one is, 'What did we do to try to achieve the objectives, what worked well and why did it work well, and what did not work well and why did it not work well?' The second one is, 'As we look back over the past three months, what lessons did we learn or relearn that can help us in the future?' The third question is, "What will we do the same going forward, what will we do differently, and why are we going to do these things?'"

Steve looked at me for a long time, and then he said, "Dan, I don't want to drive my business by looking in the rearview mirror all the time."

I said, "I don't want you to either, but if all you do is celebrate or punish people for hitting or not hitting certain results, then all you're going to do is the same thing you've always done."

Steve didn't say much more that day, but he did start to use the process. Over the next few years, even though he still celebrated a bit when his team achieved certain goals and still came down fairly hard on people when they didn't hit the numbers, he did go through the four questions in *The Raising Your Performance Bar Process* with his management team each month. During that time his organization steadily improved results in an industry that was dramatically up and down.

Now let's focus on your business and combine some of these ideas together. By regularly taking time to think you will develop a habit of reflecting and not always doing activities. When you reflect specifically on your past business objectives and your current results and you begin to dive into what worked well and what didn't work well and why that happened, you are in a much better position to make logical choices about what to do next. If you stay in constant motion and get overly optimistic or pessimistic about the future, you may keep yourself from consciously making the impact you are capable of making.

Here are the questions in *The Raising Your Performance Bar Process* one more time. I encourage you to answer these four questions once a month on your own and once a quarter with your team members all together.

1. What was your goal 90 days ago and what have you achieved today?

2. What did you do to try to achieve the objectives, what worked well and why did it work well, and what did not work well and why did it not work well?

3. Over the past quarter, what lessons did you learn or relearn that can help you in the future?

4. What will you do the same going forward, what will you do differently, and why are you going to do these things?

If you need to change the frequency, choose whatever time frame you think is most appropriate for you. There is nothing magical about the time frame or complicated about the questions. If I had asked you to put together some questions for reviewing the past quarter, you very well may have come up with something just like this or with even better questions. The challenge is in using it on a consistent basis.

When I work out, I get in better shape. The challenge is in making time to work out. The same is true with using this process. By logically analyzing what has happened and why it happened and what you will commit to do going forward, you keep emotions from clouding your decisions about the future. You can then move forward again with passion, but the activities themselves will have been logically chosen.

One key to continually improving your performance as a leader is time-spaced learning. Time-spaced learning means you learn something and then you go try it out, then after you apply what you've learned you reflect on what you did to see what you did well and what didn't go so well, then you decide on any adjustments for the next time, then you apply what you decided to do, and then you repeat this process over and over. This is the essence of *The Raising Your Performance Bar Process*.

COMPETITIVE STRATEGIES, COMPETITIVE BEHAVIORS

There has been a lot of talk lately about what countries need to do to be more competitive on the global stage. These types of conversations are about strategy. A business strategy is a statement that defines the type of business your organization is in and the type of activities the people in your company will do in the future. Strategies are important for businesses and for countries. Without a strategy there will likely be no connection between the types of activities people in the organization are doing or the types of people they are working to serve. Without a strategy guiding your organization, you will likely end up with a very weak brand, no sustainable competitive advantage, virtually no effective innovations, and very poor results.

However, even with the most brilliant strategy, you cannot compete effectively as an organization if the people in the organization are not acting in a competitive way. I don't mean competing with each other. I mean competing together to sustain a competitive advantage that matters to customers. In a moment I'm going to focus on how you can behave as a competitive business leader. I believe individual competitive behaviors can make an organization more successful. Raising the performance bar for your organization starts with individuals behaving in competitive ways.

Before I explain specific competitive behaviors, I want to point out that there are certain behaviors that some people think demonstrate competitiveness, but I argue they don't. I call these behaviors The Three Killer B's: bravado, boorish, and brutal. Bravado is synonymous with brag, bluster, and bombast, and it means a swaggering display of courage. Boorish is synonymous with uncouth, unmannered, and insensitive, and it means a coarse and blatant lack of sensitivity to the feelings or values of others. Brutal is synonymous with ferocious, gross, and rude, and means to act in a savage, cruel, and inhuman way. (Source: dictionary.com)

Bragging about your past experiences, eating like an animal, dressing like a slob, swearing like a drunken fool just because no one will tell you to stop, putting people down, and having to win every single conversation in the hallway does not make a person competitive. Repulsive perhaps, but not competitive.

Talking with bravado, acting boorish, or being brutal might intimidate other people in the short term, but they do not help the intimidator or his or her organization compete more successfully. There is a dramatic difference between intimidating people and competing successfully.

To understand competitive business behaviors, I suggest you think of a competitive situation you've been in outside of the business world. It could be sports, music, acting, academics, or some other activity where you had to compete against other people or your own past performance in order to win. You can then use insights from that activity to see more clearly how to be competitive in the business world. Here are competitive behaviors I encourage you to use as a business leader.

Define Winning

Winning in sports is very easy to understand. You get a schedule of games to play in, and then in each game you either win or lose. At the end of the season, you either win the championship or not. In practice sessions many drills are set up to immediately determine whether or not you won in a particular activity.

Winning in business is not always as short term or easy to figure out. However, in order to compete, you have to define what winning means in your role as a business leader and you have to be able to measure it. Some parts of business are easy to define in terms of winning: growing revenue, reducing cost, increasing profit, beating last year's sales numbers, adding five new customers, and so on. Other times winning in business is not as obvious, but these subtle aspects can be more important in terms of being successful over the long term. These might include improving the reliability of small parts in a product that no one ever sees, reducing the complexity of a customer's instruction guide for one of your products, or improving the impact of a presentation on an audience member's future behaviors, which can only be loosely measured by anecdotal information down the road and somewhat by his or her actual results.

I like to think about Disney's Pixar Animation Studios. It takes them four years to make a film, and then over the course of a few weekends their financial success is largely determined. Certainly they include box office receipts and DVD sales and digital video downloads as one way of defining whether or not they won, but I also believe they define winning as improving the quality of the images and the development of their characters and the impact of the message within the film.

Within your role in your organization, what would have to happen for you to be able to say you're winning? I'm not talking about your title or income or authority level. Those are by-products of winning. Increasing your salary so you can do meaningful things for other people might very well be fueling your energy at work, but that's not the type of winning I'm referring to. I'm talking about what would have to happen in terms of an outcome for your organization in order for you to say you and your team have won? If you don't know how to define a victory, how can you compete?

In order to win in business, you can't just plow through a ton of activities and work a million hours and call yourself a winner. You actually have to impact some outcome, some measure of success. What is yours?

Prepare to Win

If you're a competitor, you don't just show up and perform. You prepare as well as you can to deliver a winning performance. I think if people spent less time talking about being competitive and more time preparing to win in their organizations, they would actually compete much more successfully. Talking about winning is in-the-public-eye, exciting, and sexy. Preparing to win is behind-the-scenes, mundane, and ordinary.

Take that improved instruction manual as an example. No one in the media is going to write a front-page story about how much easier it was for customers to understand the instruction manual or how it helped the customer to assemble the product in 40% less time, but that's an example of winning within an organization that helps the business to be much more competitive in the long run. To improve the instruction manual the person might have studied the competition's materials and instruction manuals from other industries. Maybe this person prepared himself or herself by taking courses on effective writing. All of this behind-the-scenes preparation pays off in fewer customer complaints and more loyal customers.

Bring an Intense, Sustained Desire to Win

Do you show up just for the paycheck, or do you have an intense, burning desire to win within the framework of how you have defined winning at work? Athletes who win consistently over the long term have a burning desire to constantly prepare and improve within their sport.

It doesn't matter what role you have or what industry you work in. If you want to be a competitive person at work, you have to have a burning desire to do what you do as well as you can do it. I've been writing monthly articles and books on business leadership at this desk since 1998, and right now I'm trying my very best to craft a message that will hopefully have a tremendous impact on your competitiveness as a business leader. It might not help, but I have an intense desire to help you be a great business leader. What is your intense desire at work? What are you willing to compete for?

Persevere through Obstacles

Life is difficult. These are the three famous opening words from Scott Peck's book, *The Road Less Traveled*. They are powerful because they are true. On the road to winning you are going to face challenges on a daily basis. We all know that. We also all know we have to persevere in order to win. The tricky part is to actually keep going. This is where a sense of purpose comes in. You need a purpose, a reason for working, a reason to be competitive, and a reason to keep on keeping on.

What is yours? Why do you want to win at work? Do you want a greater salary so you can provide for your family and pay college tuitions and help your aging parents? Those are noble reasons to keep on keeping on. There are other reasons why people persevere. They want to leave a legacy of having mattered. They want, as Steve Jobs used to say, to put a "dint in the universe." They want to fulfill something deep inside of themselves. These are also noble reasons to keep on keeping on.

For an athlete to compete, he or she has to persevere within a practice, a game, a season, and a career. For a business leader to compete, he or she has to persevere within a meeting, a project, a quarter, and several decades. You have to keep going in order to have an opportunity to keep winning.

Are you stimulant-fueled or purpose-fueled?

One executive is driven by stimulants: salary, bonus, nicer office, company car, title, and promotions. Another executive is driven by a purpose such as making a difference in helping an organization be as successful as it can be in the short term and the long term, or to make a difference in the world with the money he or she makes.

Neither one of these people exist.

No one is completely stimulant-fueled or purpose-fueled. However, I believe the end of the spectrum you are closest to will impact your long-term performance. Stimulants are provided by someone outside of you and ultimately are all about you as an individual. They have to be continually increased in order to fuel better performances from you, or even to maintain the status quo, and even then they can eventually lose their effectiveness for driving good performances.

Purpose comes from within you and is ultimately about your impact on other people. A great sense of purpose in your work can fuel you over an entire career and continually generate greater performances.

So far in this chapter the focus has largely been about what is happening within you. What drives these internal conversations is whether you are stimulant-fueled or purpose-fueled. If your desire is to make a lasting impact as a business leader, then I believe you need to carve out some time to identify why you do what you do for a living.

Analyze Performance and Improve in the Details

Being competitive doesn't mean you have to always be performing. Sometimes, or maybe more like a LOT of times, you need to stop doing and step back and reflect on what you've done. Look at your performance and ask yourself what you're doing that is helping your chances of winning, what you're doing that is hurting your chances of winning, and what you could be doing that might increase your chances of winning.

Reflection and discernment are perhaps the two most underrated aspects of competitive business behaviors, but they are two of the most important. Rather than wasting time on acting with bravado and demonstrating boorish, brutal behaviors, I encourage you to step away from your activities and really think about what would make them even more effective.

Be Comfortable with Other People Getting Uncomfortable

On the road to trying to win you will likely encounter people who simply don't want to put in the physical or mental effort necessary to win on a consistent basis. It's okay to be honest and professional with them and to point out in a very clear way why they need to make some adjustments. This is one way your leadership skills come into play.

As I've said, business leadership means influencing how other people think so they make decisions that improve results for the organization in a sustainable way. This is another way of saying that business leadership is about competing to win.

As Tom Landry, the long-time coach of the Dallas Cowboys, used to say, "A coach is someone who tells you what you don't want to hear, who has you see what you don't want to see, so you can be who you have always known you could be." Even if you have hired competitive people, you are likely going to make them uncomfortable in some way at some point in time. That's okay. It may very well be that discomfort, alright let's call it pain, that will help them to learn how to be more competitive in the future.

If you've hired people who are not competitive and who aren't willing to learn how to compete, then you are facing a very difficult decision. Do you move forward with folks who are friendly and work hard, but who are unlikely to do what it takes to win as an organization, or do you decide to move on without them?

Competitiveness and competitive behaviors are essential elements in a winning organization. I encourage you to teach and develop competitive behaviors in your organization, but also realize that some people are not going to want to compete in order to continually improve and to press on for victory. In those cases, you have to decide what you are going to do. It's not about bravado, boorishness, or brutality. You can still maintain professionalism and integrity in whatever you decide to do.

Intelligent strategies that affect the type of business you will be in and the type of activities your organization will do in the future are important to consider carefully and to implement. However, an organization will not be competitive in the marketplace, and a country won't be competitive in the world, just because it has a good competitive strategy. What organizations and countries need are employees and citizens who consistently compete as well as they can.

There is nothing in the world that is wrong with being competitive as long as we're clear about what that means. Competitive behaviors include defining what winning means, preparing to win, maintaining a burning desire to win, persevering through obstacles, analyzing performances, and influencing other people even if it means causing them to get very uncomfortable. One caveat on competing: don't cheat. Cheating might help you "win" in the short term, but it can also ruin your career and destroy your organization. Winning only counts if you are competing in an honest way.

MANAGE YOUR PRIORITIES, NOT YOUR TIME

If you say yes to every good idea you have, you will dilute your impact on all of your ideas. You have to be willing to say no to a lot of good ideas so you have the time and the energy to say yes to the few really great ideas that will matter the most.

Susan was an executive in a medium-sized business. I was working with her as an executive coach. At three meetings in a row she told me she was working on a lot of stuff, but she wasn't getting very good results at any of it. The third time she said that to me we were sitting in a restaurant, and there were four paintings behind her.

I said, "Susan, if you were going to paint those four paintings, would you rather work on one at a time or on all four paintings simultaneously?"

She said, "Oh, I would work on all of them at the same time."

I asked, "Why would you do that?"

Without taking any time to think through her answer, she gave me one of the most honest and insightful answers I've ever heard. She said, "Well, that way I would have a built-in excuse if none of them turned out very well."

Even though that sounds funny to hear, think how often we act this way. We pile up our activities so that when someone asks how we're doing we can say, "I'm doing great. I'm really, really busy with all kinds of stuff." We say that as though doing a lot of activities equals great results. It doesn't always work that way. You have to say no to a lot of good activities so you can say yes to a few great activities in order to really make an impact.

To help you clarify your priorities and stay focused on the things that matter the most, I encourage you to answer the three questions in *The 1 – 3 - 6 Process for Focusing Your Efforts.*

1. What is the most important outcome you want to improve in your organization and why did you choose that particular outcome?

2. What three things can you personally do to improve that outcome and why did you select those three activities?

3. What six things do you need to stop doing or spend a lot less time doing so you have the time and the

energy to do the three things you know will have
the greatest positive impact on achieving your most
important desired outcome?

If you are anything like most people who have answered those three questions for me, you had very little trouble with the first question and not too much difficulty with the second question, but you ran into a lot of trouble in trying to answer the third question. That's because we were all taught to never say no to a good idea. We were always encouraged to take on as much as possible. We were told it's a sign of weakness to say we're not going to do something.

Please use this advice: stop listening to those voices in your head. You can't keep doing everything and expect to be great at anything. You have to decide in a very deliberate way what you are not going to do. Of the three questions, the third one is the most important. Take your time and answer all three of them, and really push yourself to answer the third one. The harder work is not doing things, but sacrifice allows you to be great.

I encourage you to answer these three questions once a month and keep yourself focused on doing the things that will matter the most in terms of helping you to achieve what you want to achieve. In doing so, you will consistently become more effective as a leader.

LEAD FROM THE NUMBER TWO POSITION

My hunch is that as a business leader you are in the number one position in some situations and you are in the number two position in other situations. For example, a COO is in the number one position when meeting with people from the operations staff, but is in the number two position when sitting at an executive leadership meeting with the CEO in the room. You can change the titles to fit your situation if you're not a COO, but I think you get my point. In order to be a truly successful business leader, you need to be able to be effective in the top spot as well as in the number two spot in different situations.

Be Complementary, Not Redundant

It has become clear to me that great organizations generally have two leaders at the top, and they complement one another's strengths. Walt and Roy Disney at The Walt Disney Company in the 1950s and Michael Eisner and Frank Wells at The Walt Disney Company in the 1980s and Steve Jobs and Tim Cook at Apple in the 2000s are all examples of co-leaders who complemented one another very well. Each pair had a visionary, out-front leader and a behind-the-scenes operations expert who kept the trains on the track.

The key to being a great number two leader is to complement the number one leader without being redundant on style. For example, if the top person in the group is a very vocal, hands-on, high-energy type of leader and you have that same style, then I suggest you adapt to the situation and be more of a calm observer who employees can come to for private advice. The group doesn't need two hard-drivers. They do need complementary styles. Don't change your values, just your approaches.

LEAD THROUGH MAJOR CHANGE

A few years ago I realized that in almost every client organization I was working with across multiple industries there were people who were talking about dealing with major change. A temporary change is where you deal with the change and then you go back to the old way of doing things. A major change is where you deal with the change and then on the other side of that change some things are significantly different.

In order to better understand how to lead effectively through a period of major change I decided to study leaders during periods of major change in history and look to see what they did and did not have in common. I selected the time frame of 1768 – 1968. The specific major changes within that 200-year slice of history I examined were the American Revolution, the U.S. Civil War, the Native American Indians' struggle to retain their freedom, the Women's Suffrage Movement in the U.S., World War II, the Cuban Missile Crisis, and the Civil Rights Movement in the U.S.

The books I read in researching major change were:

Thomas Jefferson: The Art of Power by Jon Meacham

Lincoln: The Biography of a Writer by Fred Kaplan

Chief Joseph: Guardian of the People by Candy Moulton

The Journey of Crazy Horse: a Lakota history by Joseph Marshall

Century of Struggle: Women's Rights Movement in the United States by Eleanor Flexnor

Churchill: The Power of Words by Martin Gilbert

One Minute to Midnight: Kennedy, Khrushchev, and Castro on the

Brink of Nuclear War by Michael Dobbs

The Autobiography of Martin Luther King, Jr. edited by Clayborne Carson

After reading these books I identified the following lessons on leading through major change.

Gender, Race, Age, Formal Education, Personality Type, Wealth, and Leadership Approach are Not Key Factors

From these moments in history you will find great leaders who were male and female, Caucasian, African-American, Native American, and English. Thomas Jefferson, Elizabeth Cady Stanton, Winston Churchill, John Kennedy, and Martin Luther King were all very well educated. Abraham Lincoln, Chief Joseph, and Crazy Horse had received very little formal education. Kennedy was very wealthy and Lincoln was remarkably poor. Jefferson did inherit a great deal of wealth, but in the end he owed everything he had to his creditors when he died. Stanton was raised in and married into very wealthy families. Kennedy and Churchill were very formal in their approach to guests while Jefferson often greeted dinner guests at the White House in his old slippers and Lincoln maintained a remarkably informal approach with almost everyone.

My research supported my earlier comment that leadership is not a label. I still have never found a label that guaranteed a person was going to be an effective or ineffective leader.

People Saw the Change Coming Long Before It Happened

By 1768 it had become clear that the British Empire and the American colonies were not going to peacefully coexist for the long term. On January 10, 1776 Thomas Paine's book, *Common Sense*, was published, which accelerated the belief that the Americans needed to separate themselves from Great Britain. This was almost exactly six months before Thomas Jefferson wrote the Declaration of Independence. Discussions on women's rights to education, property ownership, and voting began more than 40 years before the first Women's Rights Convention in Seneca Falls, New York in 1848. There was talk of a civil war happening over the issue of slavery fully 20 years before it occurred. The U.S. federal government had talked about the "Indian Problem" more than 25 years before the climactic battles in 1876-1877 between the U.S. military and the Nez Perce and Lakota

Indians. Anger over a lack of civil rights for African-Americans had been brewing for nearly a century before Rosa Parks refused to give up her seat on a bus in 1955. By the 1950s it was said that the nuclear buildup in Russia and in the U.S. could lead to a thermonuclear war, which is nearly what happened in October 1962.

By seeing a major change developing, you can better prepare your organization to successfully transverse the new terrain when it arrives. Here are two well-known examples. In the 1950s, Americans had more televisions, more leisure time, and more expendable income than at any previous time in history. By seeing these major changes early in their evolution, Walt Disney created two very successful television programs and a theme park and Ray Kroc began to build McDonald's restaurants in communities across the U.S.

What major change do a lot of people in your organization know is coming and what can you do to prepare your organization to leverage that major change into a better future?

The Leader Declared When the Critical Moment Had Arrived that Changed History

When it became clear that THE moment had arrived, Jefferson created his famous document, Elizabeth Cady Stanton wrote and published the Declaration of Principles that established the formal beginning of the movement for women's rights, Lincoln wrote the Emancipation Proclamation at the height of the Civil War, Kennedy announced a naval blockade of Cuba the day he found out the Russians had nuclear weapons on the island of Cuba, Martin Luther King, Jr. crystallized the purpose of the Civil Rights Movement with his "I have a dream" speech in 1963, and Winston Churchill made the following statement on the third day of World War II, September 3, 1939:

"We must not underrate the gravity of the task which lies before us or the temerity of the ordeal, to which we shall not be found unequal. We must expect many disappointments, and many unpleasant surprises, but we may be sure that the task which we have freely accepted is one not beyond our compass and our strength."

Think about the major change you and the members of your organization face right now. Then reread that statement and apply it to your situation. Don't underrate the gravity of the task that lies before you, your organization will not be found unequal, and the task is not beyond your compass or your strength. Those are reassuring words that clarify your capacity for dealing with this moment.

When a leader declares the critical moment that changes history has arrived, it allows people to finally confront the major change and deal with it. Until that moment happens, people can see the change coming, but they don't do anything about it. By delaying action, things don't get better. They get worse.

Is it time for you to declare the moment that changes the history of your business has arrived? If it is, then it's your responsibility to declare this is that moment so people in your organization will start to truly confront this major change. If you hesitate, you can make things a lot worse for your organization over the long term, and you might even cause your organization to collapse. If you decide you are really dealing with a major change and not just a temporary change, you hold the future of your organization in your hands. Step up and lead.

Know Your Words Matter, A Lot

When you are dealing with a major change, your words matter a tremendous amount because now people are listening more attentively than ever before.

In August 1963 before 250,000 people, Martin Luther King, Jr. said, "When the architects of our republic wrote the magnificent words of the Constitution and the Declaration of Independence, they were signing a promissory note that all men, yes, black men as well as white men, would be guaranteed the unalienable rights of 'Life, Liberty and the pursuit of Happiness.' It is obvious today that America has defaulted on this promissory note insofar as her citizens of color are concerned… There will be neither rest nor tranquility in America until the Negro is granted his citizenship rights." Those were words that stirred Americans into realizing they were all dealing with a period of major change, and people took extraordinary action to create the necessary changes.

On July 19, 1848, a frustrated housewife named Elizabeth Cady Stanton stood up to speak at the first ever Women's Rights Convention in the United States, which she had organized and attracted 250 women and 50 men to attend, and said, "I should feel exceedingly diffident to appear before you at this time, having never before spoken in public, were I not nerved by a sense of right and duty, did I not feel that the time had come for the question of woman's wrongs to be laid before the public, did I not believe that woman herself must do this work; for woman alone can understand the height, the depth, the length and the breadth of her degradation."

At the time Stanton gave this speech women in the U.S. could not own property, had to give any money they earned to their husband, had to give their children to their husband in the event of a divorce, and could not change these rules on their own because they were not allowed to vote. Her speech began the long organized battle for women's voting rights in the United States that did not occur until August 1920.

On May 13, 1940 when it was obvious that Germany was trying to annihilate Great Britain, in his first speech as Prime Minister, Winston Churchill said, "We have before us an ordeal of the most grievous kind. We have before us many, many long months of struggle and of suffering. You ask, what is our policy? I will say: it is to wage war, by sea, land and air, with all our might and with all the strength that God can give us; to wage war against a monstrous tyranny, never surpassed in the dark and lamentable catalogue of human crime. You ask, what is our aim? I can answer in one word: it is victory, victory at all costs, victory in spite of all terror, victory, however long and hard the road may be; for without victory, there is no survival."

These words stirred people's minds and hearts across Great Britain to give everything they had to succeed.

If your organization is dealing with a major change, what can you say to clarify the situation and to instill in the hearts of all of your employees a sense of purpose and drive and significance? Your words matter, a lot.

Sustain a Focused and Flexible Effort

In each piece of research I found that the major change the group was dealing with extended for many years and in most of the situations for many decades or more. The attempt for the United States to form and separate from Great Britain lasted at least from 1768 – 1812. The fight to end slavery in the U.S. formally lasted four years, but really was in the making long before that. The fight for Great Britain to retain its independence went from World War II (1939 – 1945) into the Cold War that lasted much longer with the constant threat of a nuclear war hanging over everyone's head. The even longer attempts to deal with major change were fighting for equal rights for women, African-Americans, and Native American Indians, each of which has lasted for well over a hundred years.

As you deal with a major change facing your business, be patient and persevere. The effort might even outlast your career. The key is to remain focused on the major change and to continually lean into making it a step toward a better reality.

Also be flexible in your approach to addressing this major change. Look at the variety of ways that Martin Luther King, Jr. attempted to gain equal footing for African-Americans from 1955 – 1968. He marched in non-violent protests, gave inspiring speeches from a church pulpit, met with the president of the United States, wrote a long and clear letter from the Birmingham jail, gave a really powerful and memorable extemporaneous speech on the steps of the Lincoln Memorial in Washington, D.C., served as the president of the Southern Christian Leadership Conference, wrote a variety of books, and traveled across the U.S. to get his message across.

As a business leader, what are the different ways you can play a role in guiding your organization, or your part of the organization, toward effectively dealing with the major change confronting you? If you always do the same thing in the same way, you are probably significantly limiting your impact on the ultimate outcome.

Understand the Importance of Freedom and Independence

Another common denominator of all seven major historical changes that I studied was that they were centered on gaining and maintaining freedom and independence. Over and over in multiple societies and on different continents people were willing to lose their lives if it meant helping other people to win and preserve their freedom and independence. If those two values are worth going to war over, imagine how important they are to your employees. Are you allowing your employees to maintain the freedom to think for themselves and to make independent decisions? If you're not, you may very well be robbing your organization of two of the most important characteristics required to successfully confront a major change.

Retain Your Ability to Choose

Perhaps the most horrific major change that any group of people has ever faced were the Nazi concentration camps of World War II. Millions of Jewish people were marched into a camp where they were either killed or forced to serve as slave laborers in the worst possible conditions. Yet even in this most heinous of major changes people still could retain their ability to choose how they thought about the change.

Viktor Frankl was a Jewish prisoner in a Nazi concentration camp. In his book, *Man's Search for Meaning*, he wrote, "We who lived in concentration camps can remember the men who walked through the huts comforting others, giving away their last piece of bread. They may have been few in number, but they offer sufficient proof that everything can be taken from a man but one thing: the last of the human freedoms – to choose one's attitude in any given set of circumstances, to choose one's own way…In the final analysis it becomes clear that the sort of person the prisoner became was the result of an inner decision, and not the result of the camp influences alone. Fundamentally, therefore, any man can, even under such circumstances decide what shall become of him – mentally and spiritually. He may retain his human dignity even in a concentration camp."

No matter how painful the major change your organization is facing becomes for you and your fellow employees, you still have the ability to choose how you think about this change and how you deal with it. You have the freedom to choose your attitude.

It is Healthy for a Leader to Acknowledge His or Her Fears and Confront Them

It is not unhealthy to be afraid of the future. It's unhealthy to pretend you're not afraid. Jefferson was afraid when the British soldiers showed up at his home in Virginia looking for him after he wrote the Declaration of Independence. Stanton was afraid her husband would leave her and that others would ridicule her over her stance on women's rights. Kennedy was afraid that the Cuban Missile Crisis could cause the death of tens of millions of people. Lincoln was afraid that he might be assassinated at any moment for declaring that black people should not be slaves. Crazy Horse and Chief Joseph knew their fight to retain freedom for the Native Indians could likely end their lives. Churchill knew his name was on the Nazi "People of Interest" list, which meant they wanted to kill him. King knew he could be assassinated at any moment. It's okay to be afraid of the future and what might happen to you. Here are four questions I encourage you to answer.

1. What are you afraid of as you think about the future?
2. Why are you afraid?
3. What can you do to address these fears?
4. What is your motive for taking action as you move forward?

Motivation is an internal matter. It means having a motive to take action. By acknowledging your fears and reminding yourself of your motive for dealing with this major change, I believe you will be able to move forward in the face of fear and still be effective as a business leader.

Luck Plays an Important Role in Success

Generally speaking, historical leaders became famous because they won. They succeeded in dealing with a major change and came out a winner on the other side. If they got killed along the way like Lincoln, Kennedy and King, they became even more famous, but winning was the crucial variable in determining long-term fame. In a lot of ways this is true in business as well. If you take on a major change and guide your organization to success, you are instantly proclaimed a great business leader. However, you could have been the exact same business leader and lost.

Winston Churchill is considered one of the greatest leaders of all time. The same is true with Thomas Jefferson. John Kennedy is highly regarded for avoiding a nuclear war in October 1962. However, if the Nazi Germans had not diverted their attention away from Great Britain to attack Russia and if the Japanese Air Force had not attacked Pearl Harbor and provoked the United States into joining the attack on Germany, there is a very good chance that the Nazis would have taken over Great Britain. If the British military had leveraged their enormous advantages in December 1776 instead of partying and giving the American colonial army a small window of opportunity to survive and attack, then Great Britain may very well have kept the colonies in their empire. If Fidel Castro had been able to convince Nikita Khrushchev to send a nuclear attack at the U.S. as he wanted to, then Kennedy would likely have been forced to attack Russia with nuclear weapons. Good fortune played a major role in the success of each of these leaders.

In studying Chief Joseph and Crazy Horse, I found they displayed the same courage, they held the same sense of purpose in trying to preserve freedom and independence for their Indian Tribes, and in many ways used the same verbiage as Churchill, Jefferson, Lincoln, and Kennedy. However, luck was not on their side.

After the Civil War, the U.S. military maintained a focus on removing the Indians from any truly independent way of living and forced them onto reservations. The U.S. government could have focused on taking over Canada or Mexico. That would have been similar to Nazi Germany going after Russia and taking their eye a little bit off of Great Britain, but that's not what happened. The U.S. military's size and strength was simply too much for the Native Indians to hold them off forever. Based on my research, I admire Chief Joseph and Crazy Horse for their integrity, honesty, ability to influence people in their organizations, and sense of personal dignity as much as I do any of the other leaders. The difference is they lost, and the others won.

As you work to deal successfully against a major change that is affecting your organization, you may win and you may lose. Some things are within your control, and many other things are not. Lead to the best of your ability and operate within the things you can control, but don't disparage yourself if in the end your organization collapses or fails. Success in dealing with major change requires a lot from you, but it also requires a certain degree of luck to give you the opportunity to succeed.

You have to be Near the Action

You can't confront major change from an extreme distance. Churchill traveled throughout Great Britain and to Russia and to the United States to gain support for the war efforts against Nazi Germany. Lincoln went and met with the soldiers in the Civil War and went to Gettysburg to be with the citizens who had lost so many loved ones. King walked the streets with sanitation workers and sat in the Birmingham jail and traveled around the country to instill a belief that America needed to change to become better.

Sometimes executives believe they can influence their employees completely from a remote location by using Skype and video conferencing and other high-tech digital communication tools. In reality, they can't do it successfully over the long term. You have to be with people at least periodically in order to influence those people. I asked a senior-level executive in a Fortune 100 company who lives near me in St. Louis why he traveled almost every week to his four manufacturing plants on the east coast.

He said, "We have a strategic plan and we have things we are trying to accomplish. When I ask one of my general managers how we're doing and the person says everything is fine, I say, 'Okay, let's go over to the plant and see what is actually happening.' I can't do that over Skype or through a phone call. I have to be with the person on-site."

If you're dealing with a major change, you have to be there with your team members a realistic amount of time in order to truly make an impact.

History provides business leaders with great lessons. Be willing to study great leaders from the past, and ask yourself how the insights you gathered can be applied in your current situation.

Build Teamwork that Works to Win

With great teamwork, you increase your chances of achieving sustainable profitable growth. With poor teamwork, you decrease your chances of achieving sustainable profitable growth. A team is a group of individuals who support one another toward fulfilling a meaningful purpose and achieving meaningful objectives.

There are two factors that strengthen teamwork and two that weaken teamwork. To strengthen teamwork, clarify a purpose and objectives that really resonate with the members of the group, and get people to work together in a way they really complement and support one another toward realizing the purpose and objectives. Values are beliefs that determine behaviors. In my work with teams over the past 25 years I have found there are three core values that are present in every true team. They are respectfulness, open-mindedness, and honesty.

People are respectful of each other meaning that they are full of respect for the other person even if they don't necessarily get along very well. Second, they are open-minded to the possibility the other person might have a really useful idea and to the possibility they themselves might have a great idea to offer. Third, they are honest with each other. They realize it's a waste of time to agree with someone in a meeting room, and then to walk out of the room and tell other people you disagree with what has been decided.

I encourage you to find ways to strengthen respectfulness, open-mindedness, and honesty in your organization. One way you can reinforce these values is to demonstrate them on a regular basis through your own behaviors. A second way is to provide positive recognition to the individual or individuals when they display these values.

To weaken teamwork, maintain a vague or meaningless purpose and unclear objectives that don't stir the emotions of the group at all, and get people to work against each other in separate silos.

Great teamwork and poor teamwork are very real human dynamics that are possible in every organization. One helps results, and the other hurts results.

CLARIFY A MEANINGFUL PURPOSE AND DESIRED OBJECTIVES

Rather than declaring to your group or organization what you think is its purpose, I suggest you clarify the purpose through a collaborative approach. If you tell people their purpose, then it will likely come across as your purpose for them rather than a purpose they helped to craft. There is a big difference between the two.

If the members of the group have input into developing the purpose and the primary objectives they are working to achieve, they are much more likely to take ownership of them. To that end, I suggest you gather your key team members with a range of anywhere from five to 30 people and have them answer these two questions:

1. Why does this group (or "this department" or "this organization") exist? What is the purpose this group has for being together?

2. If you are successful as a group, what would that success look like six months from now, one year from now, and three years from now?

Notice I didn't use the words "mission" and "vision." I think those words get overused in organizations and people start to roll their eyes and mentally check out when they hear them. I suggest you use these two questions instead.

Have someone facilitate the conversation so you can become a part of the group, break the group into smaller groups of five people each, give each person an opportunity to share their thoughts on each question, and then have a collaborative discussion within each small group on what they've heard. Within this discussion there can be plenty of debate and disagreement over ideas. Then someone from each small group explains to the whole group what his or her small group came up with in terms of answers to the two questions. There can be lots more debate and dialogue about what has been shared at this point. Then someone in the room takes a crack at summarizing what has been said by all of the groups.

So far, so good. The problem lies in the issues of groupthink. Groupthink is where a summary of all of the ideas is sometimes not nearly as powerful as a single great idea that could come from anyone in the group. It is up to the person in charge of the group, and I'm assuming that's you for right now, to listen to the collaborative input and then be capable of extracting an insight about the group's purpose that really resonates with the members.

The same is true for the second question about what success could look like down the road. For the second question, I encourage you to add in objectives and desired results. Be clear about what you want success to actually look like over the next three years.

Even though the group comes up with suggestions on what success could look like, it is up to the person or the executive committee in charge of the group to make the final decision. The pattern remains consistent. First, group collaboration, and then a single decision maker or a small group of decision makers craft a statement about why the group exists and what success will look like in the future.

The critical piece is that the purpose and the desired objectives mean a lot to the individuals in the group. If they don't mean a great deal to these people, you won't have a team. You will just have a collection of employees. Remember, a team is a group of individuals who support one another toward fulfilling a meaningful purpose and achieving meaningful objectives. Therefore, you have to have a purpose and objectives that truly resonate with the members of the group. Take your time in getting this right. The point is not to hang a plaque in the hallway with your mission and vision statement. The point is not to say you have it in a binder. The point is to clarify a purpose and objectives that will help the organization be successful and cause people to want to work together and really support each other toward making these into a reality.

CLARIFY EXPECTED BEHAVIORS

While you have a group working on clarifying its purpose and desired objectives, there is one more question I encourage you to have them answer: how will we work together?

If the people in the group have a say about how they will work together and they establish clear guidelines, then it will make it much easier for them to hold each other accountable to those behaviors. It becomes the group's guidelines on behavior rather than guidelines that were forced on to them. If there are positive and negative consequences for people who operate inside and outside of these guidelines and if the members of the group hold each other accountable for sticking to these guidelines, then eventually these behaviors will become the norm for the people in the group.

Establishing the norm for behaviors can help in many ways. One of these is that it will become clear fairly quickly if a person's behaviors fit the culture for the organization. I define culture as a set of consistently displayed behaviors. A culture is not what people say they will do, but rather what they actually do on a consistent basis. In some company cultures, swearing and yelling at each other are normal behaviors, and in other organizations those behaviors would be the reason why a person is fired. By taking the time to clarify the expected behaviors and getting them to become the norm, you increase the chances of finding people who fit in effectively in your organization.

FOCUS ON THE FUNDAMENTALS OF EFFECTIVE COMMUNICATION INSIDE YOUR ORGANIZATION

I was asked by a client to put together a full-day seminar on how people can communicate more effectively with other employees inside her business. My first thought was that this would be like asking a scientist for a cure for the common cold.

By far and away the biggest issue inside of organizations is the way individuals communicate with one another. I've worked now with over 200 organizations. To prepare for my work, I have many times interviewed anywhere from 10 to 20 people inside the organization to better understand their perspectives. I ask them to share their thoughts with me on what makes the organization effective, what makes the organization ineffective or gets in the way of it being as effective as it could be, and what would make it more effective.

I've now interviewed more than 800 people in these organizations, and without exception the number one answer to what gets in the way of it being as effective as it could be is poor communication within the organization. I'm not talking about communicating with customers, prospects, and suppliers. I'm talking about communicating with fellow employees.

If poor communication is so prevalent in organizations in over 40 different industries, I'm wondering if great communication is even possible. Do people really know what they want? Take out a sheet of paper and write down what great communication inside of a business means to you and what you think it looks like. You might want to think of someone you consider to be a great communicator or think of what you imagine great communication looks like in a work environment. Take a few minutes right now and start jotting down what you think this really looks like. When you're done compare your answer to the realities of your workplace. What is similar and what is different? What do you think can be done to improve communication in your organization? Trust me when I say improving communication in an organization is easier said than done.

Think of business performance this way:

$$\text{Talent + Energy + Time = Improved Results}$$

Business talent is the capacity to add value to other people, energy is the effort you put into creating and delivering that value, and time is the amount of time you concentrate your energy on creating and delivering that value to other people.

Keep in mind your organization only has "x" amount of cumulative talent, energy, and time. If you waste a portion of that on poor communication, then it's gone and can't be retrieved, and now you have to achieve great results with a smaller amount of talent, energy, and time. Consequently, poor communication makes great business performance much more difficult.

COMMUNICATION APPROACHES THAT RUIN WORK RELATIONSHIPS

In order to thwart off poor communication acknowledge what it looks like and work to consciously avoid it. To get ready for the seminar I started thinking about communication approaches that I have seen damage relationships within my clients' organizations and in organizations I've worked in. Here is what came to mind.

Don't Respect the Other Person

At the heart of ineffective communication is a true lack of respect for the other person. This could be conscious or subconscious, but either way it rears its ugly head and weakens relationships.

Lack of Time Together One-on-One

Nothing ruins relationships faster and more effectively than not spending time together. This is true in families, in friendships, in neighborhoods, and in businesses. There's something about human nature that when people are not spending any quality time together negative thoughts and assumptions about each other start to creep in and negative walls start to build up. Forget that saying, "Absence makes the heart grow fonder." Not true. Absence makes people jump to negative conclusions that may or may not be true. If you really want to hurt a relationship with a fellow employee, do everything you can not to spend any time with the person.

The Danger of Drive-By Shootings, otherwise known as The Explosion of Public Humiliation, The Evils of Email, The Terror of Texts and Tweets, and The Fear of Facebook

Imagine you're sitting in your house and a car goes by and a bullet crashes through your window and gets lodged in the wall next to you. No one is physically hurt, but an enormous amount of fear is generated. With no explanation or warning, you have been attacked. Your neighbors all start to wonder if they are in danger as well or if this is just about you.

To a somewhat lesser degree, this is what happens when a person gets intensely criticized at work with no forewarning. The person is sitting in a meeting and suddenly the boss berates the individual in front of her peers. The person is reading through emails at the end of a long day, and she reads one from the boss that tells her all the things she did wrong at a meeting with a customer. She is rifling through text messages or tweets and finds one that calls her out personally as having been a poor performer and the text or tweet has also been sent to 10 of her peers. She goes home to catch up on her Facebook postings and sees that someone has broken her trust and revealed something very confidential about her. All of these "drive-by shootings" can ruin work relationships.

Beware of the Cute and Funny

What you think is cute and funny may not be. Barb and I had accidently broken a glass pane for the light fixture outside of the front door of our house. Since it was under the roof we figured it would never get rained on. Then a bird built a nest in there, and we thought that was cute and funny and so we didn't bother it. After about three months the nest became huge. Then one day a neighbor smelled the nest burning while we talked on the front porch. Immediately I took out the nest. What we thought was cute and funny could have burned our house down

Is there something in your business you think is cute and funny that is in reality really hurting a relationship? Perhaps you always tease a certain person for having grown up in a certain location. You think it's funny and the other person smiles every time it comes up, but in fact the person is really sick of hearing it and is getting really ticked off at you. Be aware of the cute and funny.

It's Not Just "Don't Drink and Drive," It's Also "Don't Drink and Talk."

We all know it's dangerous to drink and drive. It's also dangerous to your business relationships to drink and talk. After a few drinks, or more than a few drinks, it's amazing how stupid we can sound and not realize it. What we might have said in a coherent and reasonable manner while sober can be said while we're slurring our words and falling off our chair in ways that really, really damage work relationships.

When you're getting near to the point of drinking too much, it's best to claim a headache and go back to your hotel room by yourself. Otherwise, you might really end up with a business headache the next day.

Build a Fortress around How Things are Done

My least favorite meetings to attend are the ones where the person in charge says, "We really want to hear your ideas on this topic. Please share them with us." Then another person starts to share his or her perspective and immediately the first person says, "That won't work. Who else has a thought they want to share?" Of course, everyone puts their hand down.

I cringe when I think about these situations. So much talent in the room and yet the person in charge refused to listen or consider anything that didn't originate from his or her mind and mouth.

Share Too Many Ideas Too Fast and Too Often

The Idea Machine is the person who constantly shares his or her ideas in every meeting. If you're on a committee or at a department meeting and you always are the first one to put your idea on the table and then you add on ideas to everyone else's ideas, people will very quickly roll their eyes and shut down listening to any suggestion you offer. Another problem that occurs is when this person is the boss and his or her direct reports are on the receiving end of a constant flow of suggestions and ideas. They don't know which ideas the boss is just "suggesting" and which ones he or she is expecting to be carried out.

The Devastating Energy Drain of Non-Stop Changes

Tim was the Division President of a $4 Billion Division in a Fortune 100 Company. He loved making changes. He practically thrived on making changes just before every deadline on various projects expired. Why did he do this? Because he was in charge and could get away with it. Project after project was postponed or delayed because of Tim's changes. The impact on the key business outcomes was devastating, and people on his team did everything they could to avoid him. Finally after a few years of this kind of behavior he was let go by his boss. Before you make yet another change to a project think about the impact it might have on people.

The Deadlines Don't Apply to Me Syndrome, otherwise known as The Perception of Not Caring Created by Not Responding

These are the people who are ALWAYS late on everything. If there is a deadline to fail meeting, they will fail at it. This is a remarkably effective way to ruin relationships because it not only sends the message you don't care, but it also negatively affects the work of a lot of other people.

Constant Arm-Chair Quarterbacking, otherwise known as Relentlessly Criticizing Other People

The easiest and sometimes the highest paid job is to criticize other people, especially when it's behind their back. Unfortunately, or fortunately, the Boomerang Effect comes into play to really hurt the relationship. The Boomerang Effect is created when the person being criticized finds out about it. Now the person is mad and has every reason to be mad, and thus ends another work relationship, unless there are some apologies made, and we'll get to that soon.

Tone and Volume and Attitude Really Do Matter

It's not just what you say; it's also how you say it.

Saying "Can you please help me with this report?" is quite different than "GET OVER HERE NOW AND HELP ME FIGURE OUT WHAT NEEDS TO BE DONE. YOU'RE NOT DOING ANYTHING IMPORTANT RIGHT NOW ANYWAY."

The Vacuum Created by Fake Listening and False Praise

The only thing worse than communicating disrespectfully is to pretend you're communicating respectfully and you're really not. This happens when you nod your head up and down and smile a lot and make eye contact and say things like, "That's great. Way to go. You're doing a terrific job," when in fact you aren't listening at all and you have no idea what the person has been doing. Remember The Boomerang Effect? People will eventually figure out what you're doing.

Here are two questions I would like for you to answer.

1. Which of these approaches do you feel are the most dangerous to ruining work relationships and why do you feel that way?

2. What other communication approaches have you found that really hurt relationships at work?

By understanding what hurts relationships, you have a better chance of consciously avoiding those kinds of behaviors.

COMMUNICATION APPROACHES THAT STRENGTHEN WORK RELATIONSHIPS

A moment ago I suggested business performance can be explained using the following formula:

$$Talent + Energy + Time = Results$$

Consequently, communication approaches that strengthen work relationships optimize the talent, energy, and time in an organization toward improving results. Here are a variety of those approaches.

Respect the Other Person

At the heart of building a stronger relationship with another person is truly respecting the person. If you're only working to build a stronger relationship with the person because your boss is making you do it, then you are unlikely to make any real progress.

Do you respect the person even though you might disagree with some aspects about him or her? Why do you respect the person? What is it about him or her that you admire? If you can't find something to base your respect upon, then you aren't going to put in any real effort toward strengthening the relationship.

Spend One-on-one Time with the Other Person

At the very minimum, I believe you need to spend 90 minutes of quality one-on-one time with the other person every three months. This could be at lunch or in a conference room or riding in a car or over the phone or on Skype. For those 90 minutes have no agenda and no interruptions. Turn off your cell phone if you're meeting face-to-face and get away from your emails if you're talking over the phone. Go away from your office where you won't be tapped on the shoulder with constant requests. 90 minutes four times a year might not seem like much, but I've been amazed to find out sometimes people go a decade without ever having any quality one-on-one time with a key person in their part of an organization. Then they wonder why the relationship has never gotten very strong.

I suggest you make a list of 10 key people you want to have a strong relationship with at work, and then schedule 90 minutes with each of these individuals every quarter. If you are really faithful to that, I think you will find your relationship with each of them is much stronger at the end of the year. Then continue to do that year after year.

360-Degree Respectfulness

The ultimate relationship builder is on-going constant respectfulness to the other person. This includes to the person's face, in side conversations when you bump into him or her at a conference or during a break at a meeting, and behind the person's back when you are talking about him or her to another person. You show how much you respect the person by the comprehensive way in which you demonstrate that level of respect.

Clarify and Bring Light to a Situation as Opposed to Keeping the Other Person in the Dark

Imagine you're sitting in the back of a well-lit conference room. Your boss holds up a book and says, "Could you please come here and take this book back to your seat?" That's a very simple thing to do. You just walk up, take the book, and go back to your seat. Now imagine the room is completely dark and you can't see your boss or the book and she asks you to come get the book, except this time she doesn't have it in her hand. It's placed somewhere along the wall in her briefcase. Now it's a much more complicated situation. You are quite literally searching in the dark for a book you've never seen before.

That's what it is like when a person gives very poor directions to another person. In the absence of any reasonable clarity it is very hard for the other person to be effective at all. Unfortunately, this happens a lot. To be an effective communicator, clarify what you want done and why it is so important. Make sure the expectations are clear and the obstacles are explained well so the other person can move forward with a minimum of uncertainty. This isn't always possible, but try to put as much light on the situation as you can by explaining items of importance to the other person.

Understand What Makes the Other Person Feel Important

Dale Carnegie in quoting two other people wrote, "The deepest urge in human nature is the desire to be important. The deepest principle in human nature is the craving to be appreciated." This is from his book, *How To Win Friends and Influence People*. I first read this book in 1988. Those two sentences above have remained stuck in my brain ever since. I can't encourage you enough to read this book. It is THE master class on effective communication.

Here's another sample from that book: "If you tell me how you get your feeling of importance, I'll tell you what you are." If you can understand what drives another person more than any other factor, you will have an opportunity to communicate with that person in a way that matters the most to him or her. It takes time to understand what makes the person's heart race faster. Once you know what this is for the person, you can gear your comments toward that nerve center in meaningful ways.

Totally Listen

The ultimate sign of respect is to totally listen to what the other person is saying. This shows you care about what the person considers important at that moment. For five minutes really let go of everything else in your life and totally tune in to what the person is saying and how he or she is saying it. In general, people don't listen very well to each other. I think that's a fair statement to make after all these years of watching people interact with others. Letting go of life's distractions and attentively and empathetically listening is a remarkable gift you can give to another person.

Close the Loop

One of the best ways to show you have really listened is to follow up a few days later with thoughts and feedback on what you discussed with the person. Perhaps the biggest complaint I hear about managers in almost every company is they don't close the loop. The manager asks an employee for his or her input on an important topic. The employee goes out on a limb and gives the manager five ideas. Then the employee never hears back about what is happening with these ideas.

To close the loop means the manager considers the ideas for a few days and then gets back to the employee and lets the person know what is happening with the ideas. For example, the manager might say, "Of your five ideas, we can move the first and fourth idea into action right away, but we won't be able to do ideas two, three, and five, and here are the reasons why..." Closing the loop is a sign of respect for the other person.

The Incredible Impact of Patience and Calmness

It's quite easy for people to get frazzled. There are a lot of things in life that can create tension both at home and at work. That tension can quickly escalate at work into very dramatic situations. The person who can stay calm and patient is the one who can maintain strong working relationships with a diverse set of people and help get the group from a state of tension to one of collaboration, problem-solving, and innovation.

A Willingness to be in the Moment at a Moment's Notice

This can't be every moment, but it also can't be never.

You show how much another person means to you by setting aside what you had planned for the day to be with that person. If that person is dealing with a crisis at home or at work and you let go of what you had on your agenda to step into his or her world, you are clearly saying, "You are more important to me than what I was doing." Of course, you can't do this every day for every person you know because you would no longer be getting any of your work done. However, when you do this it sends a very loud message about your priorities.

Really Apologize with Sincerity

We still are human and we still make mistakes.

When you make a mistake, even if it you intentionally made that mistake by deliberately saying something demeaning to another person, it's rarely irreversible in terms of being unable to sincerely apologize for what you did. Go to the other person, look him or her in the eye, and say, "I'm sorry for what I did. It was the wrong thing to do, and I sincerely apologize." Of course, your future actions have to support the sincerity of that apology. You can't then go berate the person again behind his or her back and expect to be taken seriously.

Walk a Day in the Other Person's Shoes

I think most complaints about people in other departments are based on not really knowing what they are doing. The comments are constant and never-ending from organization to organization that I've consulted with. It usually goes like this. When I'm interviewing someone, he or she will say, "People in other departments have no idea how hard we are working in this department and how many hours we are putting in. They don't do anything in their department to really go the extra mile, and I'm sick of being taken advantage of." I've now heard that comment from many, many people in operations, finance, marketing, human resources, sales, IT, event planning, research and development, and senior-level management.

If people in every group feel that way, there's a very good chance most people don't understand what other people are going through. One way to make some progress toward resolving all the complaining is for people to spend time in each other's roles. Then maybe the complaining will transform to greater understanding and appreciation of what other people do.

Care About the Other Person's Success

The icing on the cake of a great work relationship is truly caring about the other person's success and genuinely congratulating him or her on that success. Teamwork happens when a group of people support one another toward fulfilling a meaningful purpose and achieving meaningful objectives. The success is not just about you as an individual. It's about the success of other individuals and the group as a whole. Be just as excited for other people when they succeed as you are when you succeed.

Here are two questions I encourage you to answer.

1. Which of these approaches do you feel are the most useful to strengthening work relationships and why do you feel that way?

2. What other communication approaches have you found that are effective in strengthening work relationships?

Communication occurs in any organization with two or more employees. It's very easy to fall into negative communication habits that drain the organization of its talent, energy, and time. By consciously working to communicate in effective ways, you are increasing the chances that more of the talent, energy, and time in your organization will go toward improving results.

MEET THE COMMUNICATION NEEDS OF THE OTHER PERSON

Great coaches in sports and great managers in business understand that players and employees need to be communicated with in different ways. One size definitely does not fit all when you are communicating with people.

If you want to build an effective working relationship with a boss, co-worker, or employee, first work to understand the other person's communication needs and then work to meet his or her needs. This is also true with suppliers, customers, prospects, and board members. Before you get to the business topic, it's important to meet the other person's communication needs. If you try to skip this stage, you will likely run into problems. The person will not want to work with you and it will make the process of getting things done effectively and efficiently much more difficult.

We're going to focus on five communication needs that people have. They are:

1. How the person wants to make decisions.

2. How the person wants to learn.

3. How the person wants to receive communication from you.

4. How often the person wants to communicate with you.

5. The most important things to that person in a work relationship.

Four Types of Decision Makers

There have been many volumes written on this topic. The DiSC® Assessment is one of the best-known approaches. Over the years I've heard ideas on how people make decisions explained in many different formats including using the characters from the I Love Lucy television series. As I see it, here are the four main types of decision-makers.

Quick Decision Maker (speed, "Did I make a decision?")

Emotional Decision Maker (fun, "Did I enjoy working with the other person?")

Logical Decision Maker (logic, "Does this decision really make sense?")

Conscientious Decision Maker (clear conscience, "Did I do the right thing?")

I will describe each type of person in more detail and offer suggestions on how you can meet that person's decision-making needs.

Quick Decision Maker (The most important factor for this person is speed. The most important question this person wants to answer is, "Did I make a decision?")

Characteristics of this type of decision maker:

Very direct and straightforward. Strongly opinionated, decisive, and forceful. He or she does not want to see a lot of paperwork or take part in a lot of small talk about the weather and what movie you saw. This person wants to consider a few options and then make a decision quickly and get on to the next thing.

How to meet the personality needs of a quick decision maker:

Listen more than talk. Be direct and to the point. Expect abruptness. Provide the person with three options and ask which one he or she thinks would be most appropriate. Often the quick decision maker will choose one of the options, but then make a few changes to it. As long as the changes fit within the parameters of what you were hoping for, go along with the changes. Limit socializing and avoid small talk. Be brief, emphasize real results, and follow up with bullet point summaries.

Emotional Decision Maker (The most important factor for this person is having fun. The most important question this person wants to answer is, "Did I enjoy working with the other person?")

Characteristics of this type of decision maker:

He or she likes small talk about non-business issues. This person is very people-oriented and really enjoys getting to know you as a person and wants to talk about where you grew up, your family members, and your favorite hobbies. The emotional decision maker very much wants the business relationship to feel right. They want to get excited about working with you. They are not into paperwork.

How to meet the needs of an emotional decision maker:

Be casual and friendly. Start off with small talk. If you avoid the small talk, this person is going to feel you are just using him or her to achieve better business results and that you don't really care about him or her as an individual. Use the person's name often. Relax, smile, and engage in a fun conversation. After you've given a reasonable amount of time to small talk, find a way to shift the conversation to business. Emphasize the importance this person brings to the project. Use handwritten note cards to follow up.

Logical Decision Maker (The most important factor for this person is logic. The most important question this person wants to answer is, "Does this decision really make sense?")

Characteristics of this type of decision maker:

Logical decision makers want to move from point A to point B in very logical steps. They want to see how all of the pieces fit together before they make a decision. They listen more than they talk. They do not like quick changes. They do not want to engage in small talk. They want to analyze facts and data before they make a decision. They want to know why you are doing what you are doing. They enjoy going through paperwork.

How to meet the needs of a logical decision maker:

Keep your emotions in check. Explain step-by-step how together you will move from point A to point B. You could use a flowchart or a giant puzzle to show how all of the different components fit together. Have your explanation typed up with copies for each of you and visually walk the person through the process. Be methodical and patient. Follow up with a clear, step-by-step summary of the discussion.

Conscientious Decision Maker (The most important factor for this person is a clear conscience. The most important question this person wants to answer is, "Did I make the right decision?")

Characteristics of this type of decision maker:

This person wants to be absolutely certain that his or her decision is the right thing to do. He or she wants to follow the rules. This person likes to look at information for a long period of time by himself or herself. Several days or weeks later the conscientious decision maker will come back and present his or her decision.

How to meet the needs of a conscientious decision maker:

Keep your emotions in check. Have phone numbers and email addresses available so the other person can validate the information. Provide hard facts backed up by statistical reports. Expect the other person to want the information to be perfect. Try to be ready to provide this person with key information on any questions he or she has, but don't wing it. If you don't know the answer, don't make one up. This person will likely check up on your input. Be very patient with this person as he or she develops the decision. Give the person plenty of time to examine the information without you being present. Be sure your follow up is accurate and backed up with facts.

As you work with another person, ask yourself what type of decision maker you are interacting with. Keep adjusting your approach to more closely meet that person's decision-making needs. It's not about you getting him or her to meet your needs. The effective business leader works to meet the needs of other people.

Four Ways People Learn to Do Something

It has become abundantly clear to me that people learn in different ways. Here are four primary ways that people learn:

Reader – "Give me the information, I'll read it over, and I'll be ready."

Doer – "I'll just start doing it, and I'll learn as I go along."

Watcher – "I'll watch how other people do it, and I'll learn from them."

Discusser – "I'll discuss the work with other people and ask questions, and I'll learn how to do it better."

If you want to be effective in teaching an idea to another person, realize not everyone learns the same way. Be willing to step back from what comes naturally for you and ask the other person how he or she wants to learn the ideas. At the very least provide a variety of learning experiences for the person until you see what is best for him or her.

Even within each of these four ways to learn there are lots of subtleties that can make a difference. Some readers like to read text in words and paragraphs while others want visual cues to follow. Some discussers want one-on-one dialogue while others prefer to collaborate with 10 people simultaneously on a project. The more you understand the other person's nuances when it comes to learning, the better your chances are of creating effective learning experiences for this individual.

How People Want to Receive Communication from You

Modern technology has expanded the ways we can deliver information and interact with other people. Some people will love one mode while others will hate that approach. Here are some of the ways you can communicate with another person: face-to-face, phone, Skype, voicemail, email, texts, spread sheets, bullet points, detailed attachments, faxes, and handwritten letters. Ask the person what he or she prefers, and watch how the person reacts to communications from you. Over time you will come to understand what is best for this person.

How Often People Want to Receive Communication from You

For some folks a daily phone call is the expected behavior. For others a monthly email recap is sufficient. It's important to identify how often the other person wants to communicate with you. Communicate too little and you risk losing the relationship. Communicate too often and you risk overwhelming the person. Be on the alert to determine the right frequency for each individual, and then determine to what level you can meet that frequency.

Understand What is Most Important for the Person in a Work Relationship

Some people will tell you their whole life story in the first five minutes and other people are still guarded in their comments five years later. It doesn't make one person better or worse than the other. It makes them human. The key is for you to figure out what the other person wants in a work relationship with you. Here are some of the things I've seen that people want: meaningful conversations on important life topics, a sense of camaraderie, having fun and laughing a lot, honesty, achieving remarkable results together, a sense of adventure, and a confidante. Nobody wants all of these things. Different people want different things from a professional relationship. The keys are to figure out what each person wants and try to meet those needs.

Of course, you will have to decide if you can talk about what the other person wants to discuss. Sometimes you won't be able to. I have had people tell me extremely private details about situations related to their sex lives that I really did not want to talk about, or hear for that matter. I quickly moved on in the conversation and didn't look back. You have to decide where you will draw the line.

Key Points to Remember

There is no magic formula or silver bullet or psychological test that can tell you exactly how best to meet the other person's communication needs in every situation. All you can do is try to figure out what is the most effective way to meet the person's needs at that moment. Here are a couple of things to keep in mind.

There is no best set of communication traits in business. You can be a great business leader as a quick decision maker who wants to only communicate once a month via bullet points or as a logical decision maker who wants information every day and expects a weekly face-to-face meeting to discuss how all of the pieces make sense in terms of improving key business outcomes. Don't fall into the bad habit of deciding whether or not a person can be a great business leader just because of his her specific communication needs.

People usually have a primary and a secondary decision-making approach, learning approach, favored way of communicating, desired frequency of communication, and sense of what is important in a work relationship. Rarely is anyone a pure logical doer or just a quick reader.

A person's communication needs can change based on the situation he or she is in at that moment. Be aware of the context of the situation. Here are five questions for you to consider when you are communicating with another person related to context. Is it a time to be serious or laid-back?

1. What's the time frame for making a decision?
2. What is happening in the other person's life?
3. What is happening in this person's part of the business, in your industry, and in the world right now?
4. What other aspects of the situation are important to keep in mind?

I had two speeches at an all-day leadership conference in Orlando. One was at 10:30 AM and one was at 4 PM. In the first session, the group was enthusiastic and positive and upbeat. At lunch that day I found out that the Boston Marathon had been bombed and that several people at the conference were worried about their family members. Suddenly it became time for me to be more serious and to give people more time in sharing their thoughts on leadership.

How You Want to be Communicated With

Before you try to understand the communication needs of other people, start with yourself.

Based on everything that was explained in this chapter, and things I didn't get into, how do you prefer to be communicated with? Try to describe your communication needs in detail. Here are seven thought-starter questions.

1. What is your primary and secondary decision making personality?
2. What is your primary and secondary approach to learning?

3. Do you prefer Skype, email, texts, face-to-face, or phone conversations? When do you like each of them? How often do you want to be communicated with?

4. What is most important to you in a work relationship?

5. Do you like to make decisions quickly or do you prefer to study a lot of information and take longer to make a decision? When do you prefer one over the other?

6. Do you like to get to the point quickly or do you prefer to engage in some small talk?

7. How long do you prefer to plan before executing a project? Six months, six weeks, six days, six hours, or six minutes?

Now write a description of your communication needs. Don't hesitate. Start writing it down now. It's important to understand yourself.

How You Think Another Person Wants to be Communicated With

As you think about people you work with, select an individual and write down how you think this person wants to be communicated with. Observe how the person reacts to different approaches from you and from other people. Be on the alert to better understand the person's communication needs, and make adjustments in how you communicate with him or her.

YOUR FUTURE DEPENDS ON WHO YOU SELECT

News Flash #1: The people you choose to hire will be the single most important factor in the future success of your career.

Okay, maybe it's not quite that dramatic, but I encourage you to take people selection very, very seriously. Of all the things you will do at work in the next six months, hiring the right people will be one of the most important. Here are six keys to keep in mind.

You are Hiring Behaviors

When you hire someone, you are hiring his or her behaviors. People really don't change as much as we think they are going to. The way a person has consistently acted over the past five years is going to be how he or she will consistently act in your company. Are the person's behaviors what you want in your business?

If you think values and behaviors are just fluff, let me put it this way. Imagine you are not allowed to fire this new hire for at least five years. Now imagine everyone knows you hired the person. Consequently, every person who interacts with your new hire is going to see this person's behaviors as representative of you for the next five years. Are you comfortable having this person whom you are about to hire represent you to everyone in your company and to every supplier and every customer? Are the values this person demonstrates in alignment with the values you believe in?

Regardless of how technically strong or experienced this person is, if you are not okay having him or her represent you to other people then I suggest you don't hire the person. There are an incredible number of talented people you could hire. You should always be choosy in who you add to your team.

Technical Skill Does Matter

Sometimes managers get so caught up in hiring the "right kind of people" they forget the person has to do a job once he or she is hired. Know which technical skills are most important for each role in your organization. Then develop interview questions, case studies, and role plays to help determine if the individual has the necessary knowledge and skill to do the technical aspects of the job.

You only get to hire so many people. Each new hire is critically important for the short-term and long-term success of both your business and your career. Make sure the person you're hiring can actually do the job you are hiring him or her to do.

Complementary Team Player

Look at your current team members. Is this new hire going to add some complementary strength to your team, or is the person going to be a repeat of what you already have? If you have a team of good listeners who are great at covering the details but who are uncomfortable bringing in new business projects, do you really need one more person just like that? Why not search for someone who is different than what you already have? If everyone is extroverted, would your group benefit from someone who is really willing to listen to a variety of opinions and then respond in a thoughtful and logical manner?

Think through not just what the individual brings to your team, but also consider the ramifications of adding this particular set of strengths and communication traits to the group as it stands right now. You might want someone who is just like the other members of the group. Maybe you want every team member to be a hard-charging, outgoing salesperson. Perhaps you have decided that bringing in someone who is dramatically different than the members of your team would be a catastrophic move. On the other hand, you might feel diversity is of great value in building the business in a sustainable manner. You have to make the call.

Do a Passion Audit

Behaving the right way and having the ability to do the job will increase the chances the person will do at least an okay job. Of course, doing just an "okay job" is not going to help your business achieve great results in the future. You need people who are both competent in and passionate about the role you are going to give them.

A time-honored interview question is, "What are you good at doing?" One of my favorites is, "What are you passionate about doing?" One of my clients asks that question of every potential new hire. If the person is not passionate about anything, then my client questions whether the person will bring real passion to working for his company.

Ask the person, "Why us? Why do you want to work here? What is it about our company that you like?" You will see very quickly if the person has any real passion for your organization and/or the role he or she is being considered for. Without passion, what are the odds of the person delivering the kind of performance that will make your organization more successful in the future? My hunch is the odds are very, very low.

Avoid Easy Hires Just Because They are Easy

There is a constant temptation to help out friends and family members. Those are the individuals who very well may have helped you get through difficult times in the past. However, just because you know them very well doesn't mean they are necessarily the best individuals to hire. They may have passion to have a job, but they may not have passion or competency for the job you are filling right now.

Sometimes good friends or family members make outstanding employees who dramatically improve business results. However, those examples are generally true when friends or family members start a business. To have a family member reporting to you in an organization that you don't own leaves open the possibility to a lot of problems. If the person has exactly the values, technical skills, and passion you are looking for, don't pass up a great talent just because you might have problems. The key is to make sure the person really has what you think he or she has and you're not just hoping for something that doesn't really exist.

Be Patient in Your Talent Search

Just because you suddenly have money to go out and hire some new talent doesn't mean you have to go do it right away. Take your time and hire the right person for the job. Rushing decisions just for the sake of short-term expediency is part of what gets companies into economic messes. Take your time and hire the right person. This person will dramatically affect the future success or failure of your career and your organization.

RELEASE TOXIC HABITS

Teamwork is a critical business driver. It affects execution, innovation, and branding. Toxic habits are anything a person says or does consistently that weakens teamwork in an organization. There are three important steps to releasing a toxic habit.

Step #1: Awareness

By raising our level of self-awareness, we begin the process of releasing our toxic habits. When we do something often enough, we turn it into a comfort zone. We break the negative comfort zones by becoming aware of them. We can't comfortably go back to our old behaviors with this new level of self-awareness.

When I first graduated from college and I was going to Happy Hours with my co-workers, I would gossip about other people. If I was with one group, I would talk badly about people in another group, and if I was with people in the second group, I would talk badly about people in the first group. I thought by tearing other people down I could make myself look better in the eyes of my co-workers. I thought wrong. All I did was pull myself down. Once I realized what I was doing I could no longer comfortably talk badly about a co-worker.

Step #2: Acceptance

We further move toward releasing a toxic habit by accepting it as part of who we currently are. If we deny having it, it will continue to control us. I had to accept the reality that I was the one who was saying rude things about other people. I knew other people were doing it as well, but this didn't change the fact that I was putting people down. Once I accepted I was responsible for this action, then I knew I had to do something about it.

Step #3: Action

Here are some ideas to consider on your road to releasing your toxic habit.

Take time to experience and express your negative emotions. If you are angry at someone and that anger is causing you to say or do toxic things, then write a letter to the person that allows you to get all of your anger on to the paper. When you're all done, tear the letter up or delete the email and either rewrite it without all of the anger or let the situation go. The key is to get the toxic emotions out of your system.

Mentally detach yourself from the end result. If you are getting so caught up in achieving a certain result that you are saying things or acting in a way that is hurting teamwork, then stop focusing on the outcome. Focus on improving the process to achieve the outcome.

If you are constantly recalling a negative memory about something you did or something that someone else did that is causing you to carry that negativity into group situations, then forgive yourself for the mistakes you made and other people for the mistakes they have made. Until you consciously let it go, the memory of those words or actions may cause you to say or do something that hurts teamwork.

In his book, *Good to Great*, Jim Collins wrote about Level 5 Leaders. These were people who maintained a high level of personal humility and a fierce resolve to help the organization succeed. In order to avoid toxic habits, remain humble so your ego does not get in the way of your decisions, behaviors, and interactions with other people.

When a person becomes overly busy and stretched beyond any reasonable limit, toxic habits have a tendency to creep into the individual's life. I encourage you to reduce the complexities of your life as much as possible. In doing so, you will have the energy stored up to deal with the occasional complexities that pop up as opposed to the non-stop complexities that exhausted people tend to create.

In the end, the key is to replace this toxic habit with a more life-enhancing habit. Once you've become aware of a toxic habit and you've accepted you really are the person who is saying or doing this destructive thing, then you need to replace it with a new action. If you try to stop an old action and not replace it with any new behavior, the old behavior will eventually work its way back into the vacuum you've created.

This is what I had to do. When I was tempted to say a negative thing about a co-worker who wasn't at a gathering, I had to learn to hold my tongue, pause, and then either say something nice about the person or change the subject. If I had tried to do nothing, I could have easily been pulled back into gossiping about the person.

THE TEAM IMPACT REALITY CHECK

One way to increase your impact as a business leader is to be an effective member of the team. This requires continually reflecting on your performance and discerning what you do that enhances teamwork and what you do that hurts teamwork. Teamwork is a group of individuals who support one another toward fulfilling a meaningful purpose and achieving meaningful objectives. The three core values of teamwork are respectfulness, open-mindedness, and honesty. I'm closing this chapter with three questions and exercises for you to consider.

1. What are you doing to strengthen teamwork in your organization? Write down what these habits are. Describe how these habits enhance teamwork.

2. What are you doing that weakens teamwork? Write down what these habits are. Describe how they hurt the team.

3. What habits will you replace the toxic habits with? Write down what new habits you want to implement and why you selected them.

DRIVER #3 EXECUTION

Execute to Achieve Your Desired Results

Execution is accomplishing what you planned.

Execution is not developing a strategy or a plan. It is doing what you planned to do. If you execute well and don't get the desired results, then you need to reexamine your strategy and plan to see what can be improved. If you don't execute well and don't do a good job in finishing off what you planned, you don't really know if the strategy or the plan would have worked.

You cannot consistently improve results and generate sustainable profitable growth without great execution. Great execution does not guarantee great results, but you cannot consistently achieve great results without great execution. You need a great strategy plus a great plan plus great execution in order to have the opportunity to consistently achieve great results.

On my bookshelves I have nine books on strategy totaling more than 2,500 pages. Good golly, is it really that complicated? A strategy is a statement that defines the type of business your organization is in and the type of activities the people in your company will do in the future. A fancier way to say this from strategy guru Benjamin Tregoe is "a strategy is the framework which guides those choices that determine the nature and direction of an organization." This is from his book, *Top Management Strategy*. From the strategy, you establish tactics and a plan of action. This plan becomes your roadmap for the entire organization to follow.

I believe the breakdown on the road to better results for organizations is almost always with execution. This is true for two reasons. One, poor execution can keep a great strategy and plan from fulfilling their potential. Two, poor execution keeps executives from really understanding how to improve their strategy and plan. It keeps them from knowing what they need to know to make things better.

As I go through these next four topics of execution, I think you will see both poor and great execution can be traced back to aspects of leadership and teamwork. In the next two chapters on innovation and branding, you will see the same pattern. Great innovations and strong brands as well as poor innovations and weak brands can also find their roots in the leadership and teamwork in the organization.

DETERMINE WHO IS GOING TO DO WHAT WHEN AND WHY THAT NEEDS TO HAPPEN

You are in charge of a group of people and you have the responsibility to achieve certain results. You have decided, or someone else has decided for you, on the type of business you are in and the type of activities people in your organization will do. You, or someone else, have decided on which products and services your organization will offer to your customers. Now you and other members of your organization need to execute.

Write down a list of the names of every employee you have. If you have too many employees to do that effectively, write down the name of the group or department or function that represents large numbers of these people. Their manager can break down these groups into individual names and responsibilities later on.

Answer this question, "Who is going to do what when and why is that going to happen?" Make sure every employee, or group of employees, has a clear role. On a piece of paper write down the responsibilities for each role and put the name of an employee or group of employees next to the role. Write down on a calendar a draft of when the various activities need to happen. Look at these documents you've just created. Think about the roles you have placed the individuals and groups in and the timeline you have created. Does it make sense to you? Do you believe this approach will help you to achieve the desired objectives? Is it clear why you want these things done and in this order? If it's not clear to you, it definitely won't be clear to other people.

Keep thinking through the responsibilities and the timeline by asking yourself, "Are these the key items for us to focus on, do I have the right people working on them, and is this the right order to do them in?" Make adjustments until you feel you have your plan as strong as you can make it. Be sure everyone in your organization has a clear role you will be able to explain. Depending on the size of your organization, you may need to work in a collaborative way with a few other key executives or managers to hear their insights and concerns before you finalize your plan.

Once you've decided who is responsible for doing certain functions and the order in which those functions need to happen and you know why you want it done this way, your next job in executing effectively is communication.

As a business leader, most of your job includes your ability to communicate with other people. When you explain the plan for execution, there are a few key concepts to keep in mind.

Communicate Clearly

When you're done talking did the other person or the other people understand what you said? One way to find out is to say, "Please state in your own words what you heard me say." If their remarks don't match yours, don't blame them by saying, "You're not listening." Instead say, "Okay, I realize I need to say that more clearly because that's not what I meant." Then explain your thoughts again with greater clarity. If a person doesn't understand his or her role or doesn't understand someone else's role, then keep the discussion going. The main goal at this point is for people to understand what is being communicated. They may not agree with it, but they have to understand it.

Communicate Calmly

If you get overly intense, the other person will not hear your message because they will be tuned into, or turned off by, your expressions and the tone of your voice, and they won't hear the actual words you are saying. If you stay calm, the other person can focus on what it is you're saying rather than on how you're saying it.

Communicate Conversationally

Just talk the way you normally talk in a conversation. If you take on a different persona or a different tone or a different vocabulary when you communicate with other people, they are going to wonder why you're not just being yourself.

Communicate Consistently

If one day you say you are all about customer service and the next day you say your number one priority is bottom-line profit on every sale, you will confuse people. If you yell one day and whisper the next, people will wonder what's going on. Just be yourself on a consistent basis and give clear input in a conversationally calm manner.

Provide Freedom in Executing Tactics

Once you've clarified who is going to do what when and why that is going to happen, then you have be okay with stepping out of the way. This is very important. Making decisions and communicating your decisions are very important in the planning process. However, if you don't give people the freedom to decide how to do their responsibilities, then you will be seen as a micromanager and a controlling boss. There may have been a time when employees were okay with bosses telling them what to do every minute of the day. I would say that time passed many years ago. The best plans are ruined by micromanagers. You need to give the people you've hired the room to make decisions about how to execute their tasks. It may not be the way you did it, and it may turn out even better than what you would have done.

Implement, Evaluate, and Adjust

Of course, once you set the wheels-of-execution in motion, you aren't permanently removed from the work. Periodically you need to evaluate both the performances and the results. Are the various employees implementing the responsibilities they were given in the order you decided on? In other words, are they following the plan? Are they getting the results you had hoped to achieve through executing the plan?

This is not micromanaging. You are trying to determine if the plan is being followed and if the results are being achieved. You might find the plan is not being executed properly, which might mean you will need to get various people back on the original track. On the other hand, you might find that the original plan needs to be adjusted. You can only determine this by evaluating individual and team performances and keeping a close eye on the results that are produced.

Hold Individuals and Groups Accountable with Positive and Negative Consequences

As the leader of the group or organization, you want to reinforce desired behaviors and change undesired behaviors. When you see people executing the plan with excellence, provide them with positive consequences. Those can range from a pat on the back to public praise to bonuses and increased compensation. When you see people doing a poor job of executing the plan, provide them with negative consequences. Those can range from a private conversation to a formal write-up to reduced compensation to letting the person go.

Keep in mind the rationale for providing consequences is to affect habits and ultimately improve the organization. You're not just trying to rectify a situation one time. You're trying to influence how the person thinks about his or her approach to the work and how he or she will consistently act in the future.

Continually Re-clarify Who is Doing What When and Why That is Happening

It's very easy for roles to get blurred and people to get confused. Then you add in retirements and new hires and promotions and suddenly what once was clear is no longer clear. At least twice every year bring your team together and communicate who has what role and why that is the case. It may feel like you're overdoing it, but the reality is there will be some people out there in your organization who are confused about roles and responsibilities. Then feelings get hurt and drama rises and time gets wasted and productivity goes down and execution is hurt.

DEAL EFFECTIVELY WITH PROBLEMS

A problem in execution is when a process that consistently produced a certain result in the past no longer achieves the same objective. The current "poor performance" can end up wasting a lot of time, money, and energy while you're trying to accomplish what has been planned. The key is to stay logical and not get emotional.

Apply Comparisons to Solve Problems

Take the time to compare the details of what was done previously to generate the result to the details of what was done this time that did not produce the same thing. Something is different. Perhaps a key step has been overlooked or a machine part has worn out or the market has changed in some significant way. Any of those changes could be keeping your organization from reproducing the desired result. Once you identify what is different from the past, then you can fix one element at a time and test the process again to determine if it was the needed change to reproduce the desired result. It's possible you may have to create a new process in order to generate the same result you achieved in the past.

Understand Why Problems Don't Get Solved

I just explained a process approach to solving problems. While it may take quite a while to locate the process problem and fix it, this is relatively simple compared to the issue of people not wanting to deal with the problem.

In his book, *Collapse: How Societies Choose to Fail or Succeed*, Jared Diamond wrote "the most frequent reason that societies fail is that they fail even to attempt to solve a problem once it has been perceived." He explains two primary reasons why people choose not to solve a problem that they know exists. He calls these "rational behavior" and "irrational behavior."

A rational approach to making a decision that hurts execution is when a person makes a decision that advances his or her best interests, but is potentially harmful to other people. More mundane descriptions of this behavior are selfishness, self-centeredness, and greed. When the individual is rewarded in the short term for doing something that can hurt the organization over the long term, he or she can rationally think the best thing to do is to win in the short term because he or she may not be around in the long term.

For example, if a salesperson earns a bonus for making a massive sale that causes operations to invest millions in overtime pay and the organization to lose money, he or she wins while the organization loses. On a broader scale, elected politicians in the U.S. rationalize creating enormous federal debt possibly because they believe they won't be reelected if they change federal programs in any meaningful way. Consequently, they keep their jobs and forfeit away much of the potential future success for later generations of Americans.

An irrational behavior is when a person realizes there is a problem that is bad for him or her as an individual and bad for the organization, but chooses to do nothing about it. As Diamond explains, this can happen for a variety of reasons.

There could be a conflict of values. People might continue to do something they know is harmful for everyone involved because of their long-standing values. For example, taking care of the poor and elderly has long been considered a noble thing to do in the U.S. So Americans justify going farther and farther into debt as a country even though they know at some point the national debt will cause enormous pain for everyone in the country, and possibly even a collapse.

The decision maker could get caught up in groupthink or "crowd psychology." If you are leading the execution team and you're five days away from hitting a major deadline, you and others might get caught up in the moment and ignore obvious warning signs that just popped up about an unforeseen danger.

You could be psychologically worn out and not have the energy to take on another battle within the project with your boss or your boss's boss. You may have gotten to a point where the pain of a failed project is less than the pain of having to fight with your boss. Subconsciously you know there is going to be a great deal of problems for you and others down the road, but you just don't want to deal with another difficult conversation right now.

The first step to addressing these problems of rational and irrational behavior is being aware of them, and the second step is accepting they really can happen in your organization. This will help you to stay on the alert and be willing to address them. This is why it's so important to oversee the execution in your organization. Here are a few questions to keep in mind when your group is in the execution phase.

1. Are people making decisions that are best for the organization both in the short term and the long term?

If not, it may be up to you to intervene and reverse a decision. This is a difficult and delicate move to make, but it's important to remember that another person's rational self-interest can ruin execution.

2. If there is a clash of values, are you bringing people together to openly discuss those values in order to determine which ones should be guiding the execution of the plan?

3. If people have fallen into groupthink or gotten caught up in the rush of finishing a project on time, are they avoiding problems that will damage the organization in the long term?

Again, it may very well be up to you to step in and say, "I appreciate your desire to finish this project on time. However, are there difficult decisions that you are avoiding right now that could come back to really hurt our business in the future?" Just by calling this issue out in the open, you can get people to talk about the ramifications of their decisions. In this way people can take some time to discuss the short-term and long-term benefits and problems of proceeding forward with the decision.

LEVERAGE YOUR RESOURCES TO ACHIEVE SUSTAINABLE SUCCESS

Sustaining success is THE great challenge of our generation.

Every generation has taken on some great cause and left its mark on history. In the 1930s and 1940s our ancestors took on the challenge of the Great Depression and World War II and guided us through an extraordinary advance in education. In the 1950s, 1960s, and 1970s wise and courageous people took on the issues of civil rights and have generated extraordinary progress in creating greater opportunities for more people just in my lifetime alone. Over the past 30 years a technological revolution has allowed people around the globe to communicate with each other in real time and advanced our lives in countless ways. During that same time advances in medicine have significantly increased the average life span and the quality of life for millions of people.

However, throughout the centuries we still have not figured out how to sustain our successes and build on them. We operate as though age-old myths dictate our decisions. We've been told forever that for every up there must be a step down and success is cyclical and beyond our control. We seem to think improving our performance and results in a sustainable way is a foolish, idealistic notion.

But why have we given in so easily? Why can't we make the central focus of this generation the search for ways to build on past successes and increase momentum toward our desired outcomes? This is just as important for individuals and small groups as it is for organizations and societies.

You have resources for sustaining success you can turn to over and over again. In doing so, you can successfully build on your earlier achievements and continually improve your performance and results.

Resource #1: Your Definition of Success

Take out a sheet of paper and write down your definition of success. What does achieving success mean to you?

My definition of success is bringing a vision into reality. Since I get to choose the vision I want to bring into reality this allows me to not get caught up in what other people consider to be success. If I am working with another person to clarify the desired vision, then I have chosen to co-create what that picture of success looks like with this individual or group of people. However, we are creating the desired vision and not allowing other people to impose their standards on us.

What does success mean to you? What is your definition? Think about the different areas of your life both on an individual basis and in terms of the organizations you are a part of. Write down specifically what you consider success to be for each of the different aspects of your life.

Resource #2: Your Time

You get 24 hours to do what you want with. If you want to let other people dictate how your time is used up, that's up to you. Just know time is one of your resources for continually improving your results. The way you use it will determine to a large degree whether or not you sustain your earlier performances and go beyond them.

Resource #3: Your Choices

Sustaining success is just as much about avoiding the stupid, debilitating decisions as it is about proactively selecting the moves that generate better results. If you look at the wild economic swings the world has experienced just since 1990, you can see where poor decisions led many people to a financial breakdown whether it be in the housing market or the dotcom bubble mania or some other area.

Here's a suggestion. Before moving into action or making a purchase or investing in an idea, ask yourself, "Will this decision bring only a short-term gain or will it increase my chances for sustaining my current success and building on it in the future?" There are no crystal balls, but pausing to reflect on this question may help you avoid stumbling backward.

Resource #4: Your Integrity

A subset of your overall choices directly involve your integrity. As I look back on the timeframe since 1990 it seems to me most collapses for enormously successful people can be traced to financial fraud or cheating on a spouse. I suggest you could go back several decades, and maybe even centuries, before 1990 and find the same pattern. In other words, successful people interrupted their ability to sustain their results by choosing to cheat. Perhaps they lost sight of what they wanted in the first place or decided they wanted shortcuts to increase their "success." Whatever the reason, letting go of their integrity greatly diminished their chances for sustained success. This is one way people ruin execution in their organizations. Everything is moving along beautifully, but then a key member has to be removed for a lack of integrity and it hurts the team performance.

When you maintain your integrity, you can start each day with a clear conscience. That alone can help you to sustain success over the long term. When you lose your integrity, you're done, and eventually your results will prove it. Before moving into action, ask yourself, "Do I believe this is the right thing for me to do?" For your organization, ask yourself and others, "Do we believe this is the right thing for us to do?" Pausing in order to maintain integrity can have an enormous upside over the long term.

Resource #5: Your Capacity to Earn Your Results

If you blame others or something outside of yourself for your results, it may feel good in the short term, but it might keep you from taking hold of your results for the long term. On the other hand, if you ride some short-term advantage such as being in a hot industry to great results today, you may find that the advantage is not sustainable.

I encourage you to always take responsibility for your results regardless if they are good or bad. In doing so you can see what adjustments you need to make in order to steadily improve results.

In her books, *The Fountainhead* and *Atlas Shrugged*, Ayn Rand coined a phrase called "Second-Hand People." These are the people who gain results off of the efforts of other people. Throughout these books she highlighted the importance of preserving the right to earn your own results. She emphasized not giving away the responsibility for your results to some group outside of yourself. When you do that you give up your ability to guide your results over the long term, and then you lose your ability to achieve sustainable success. No matter how tough times get don't relinquish your capacity to earn your results.

Resource #6: Your Purpose

In studying very successful individuals for over 25 years, one common denominator I have found is they all had a clear purpose they held on to for an extended period of time. These individuals knew why they were doing their work. Without a clear and compelling purpose for doing your work it is unlikely you will maintain the energy necessary to continually improve your results. The fundamental question you need to answer is, "Why am I doing this? What is the purpose behind my activity?" If you can't find a compelling reason for doing what you are doing, you need to move on to an activity you can find deep purpose in doing.

Resource #7: Your Strengths and Passions

I'm convinced you can take away all of the trappings of success from a great performer, and he or she will generate as great or greater success in the future as long as you leave the person his or her strengths and passions. However, if you take away the person's strengths and passions while leaving the trappings of success in place, the person will soon lose all of the indicators of success.

Your strengths and your passions are a big part of your engine for generating sustainable success. Be sure to be highly aware of what you are good at doing and what you are passionate about. Then spend as much of your time and your energy as you can using your strengths and your passions to fulfill your purpose and drive better results. It's the simple formula I mentioned in Chapter One that great performers have used for centuries to continually achieve higher levels of performance. Your strengths and passions are at the heart of your ability to execute at a very high level.

Resource #8: Your Past Experiences

Rather than looking at a past experience as an isolated event, think of it as one step in an overall journey of successes and failures. If you look back at the important events in your life and extract valuable lessons, you can add those insights to your repertoire for improving your decisions going forward. Consequently, every past event, success or failure, becomes a valuable resource for you to increase your successes going forward.

Don't think of achieving sustainable success as some outlandish, pie-in-the-sky wish. Instead think of it as a process that has to be carefully watched over and executed with discipline. You will steadily get better and better at achieving a result and then finding ways to equal or improve this result in the future.

HOW TEAMWORK IMPROVES EXECUTION

Again, a team is a group of individuals who support one another toward fulfilling a meaningful purpose and achieving meaningful objectives.

Move from Conflict to Collaboration

A conflict is when two people disagree over something and they fight each other in an attempt to win one side of the argument. Collaboration is when two people exchange ideas and discuss how to improve them in order to come up with better ways to achieve the desired outcome.

Conflict in an organization is oftentimes unrelated to the issue being discussed. The two people are physically or mentally tired or frustrated over something, and then they come into a discussion on how to solve some problem. Rather than collaborating and exchanging ideas on how to solve the problem in an objective manner, they start to compete with one another in an emotional way to see who can "win" and do things their way.

You don't resolve conflicts. In a true conflict the two opposing forces fight until there is a victor and a vanquished. The key is to move to collaboration. For this to happen, both parties involved need to see the value of collaborating. They need to see that they can come up with better answers and achieve better results by exchanging ideas, listening to one another, and working to enhance the quality of the ideas. They need to value a better business outcome more than winning a conflict.

Here's a simple exercise that shows the difference between conflict and collaboration. Choose a topic. For example, the internet. Now make two opposing statements like "the internet is the best thing for teenagers" and "the internet is the worst thing for teenagers." Then have one person argue in support of the first statement and one to argue in support of the second statement. At this point, each person is only seeing the topic from one perspective. Then have them work together to support the first statement and then have them work together to argue in support of the second statement. By working together to argue both sides of the issue, they will help each other expand their understanding of the issues involved.

Then have them do the same thing with a work issue. First, they work together to argue for one approach and then they work together to argue for the opposite approach. In doing so, they help each other to expand their understanding of what they are facing. The key here is to get them to see the value of collaborating and the downside of conflict. Then they can work together to solve the problem by answering this question, "What can we do to solve the problem?"

Give Candid Feedback about Poor Performances

A poor performance is one that hurts execution and diminishes the end result. Candid feedback is honest input based on observations of a poor performance. Giving someone candid feedback is an act of leadership and an essential part of improving execution. Here are some thoughts on the don'ts and do's of candid feedback.

Don't give it for your glorification or gratification. Don't give someone candid feedback to make yourself look better or feel better.

Don't give it in front of other people if at all possible. The point is not to embarrass the other person. The point is to help the person understand what he or she is doing that is hurting execution.

Don't give it via e-mail, text, or voicemail. As I mentioned earlier, these are drive-by shootings that damage relationships.

Do give it for the other person's future success and for the good of your organization. Your giving candid feedback in order to help this person succeed and to help the organization be more successful. Keep this in mind at all times.

If at all possible, do give it in private, either face-to-face or over the phone. Sometimes that's not realistic and you have to give the candid feedback in front of others, but I encourage you to keep that as a last option.

Do give it based on observed behavior, not hearsay. It is possible that a few other people just want to get rid of this person, and they are making things up. Try your best to observe the person in action before giving him or her negative feedback.

Do give the person sufficient time to hear your thoughts, reflect, and respond. It's not, "Here's my feedback for you," and then you walk out of the room. Instead make sure the person has some time to think through what you've said and to respond to you.

Do meet with the other person again on the topic. Candid feedback requires multiple conversations. If you really care about this person's future success and the future success of the organization, be willing to meet with the person again in a few weeks to discuss how things have gone since you gave the candid feedback.

Reasons Why People are Not Candid

Even though candor is important in terms of improving execution, some executives and managers still tend to avoid the difficult conversations about poor performances. Here are five statements I've heard an executive or manager say as to why he or she is not being candid with the employee. My response to the individual is below the statement.

"I'm too busy."

What about the time you will spend on this situation later on by not dealing with it now?

"I only have to work with this person for one more week."

Yes, but someone else will have to work with this person next month and next quarter and the year after that. How much time and energy is going to be wasted if this person continues to be ineffective in some way?

"It's faster to just do it myself."

That's true the first time, but what about when you have to do it over and over? You basically are paying a person to do a job, and then you are doing the job yourself. That is a very inefficient use of time and money, and it is hurting execution in your company.

"I might hurt the other person's feelings."

How much will the person's feelings be hurt when a year from now he or she doesn't get promoted or does get fired because of a behavior you didn't mention?

"It's uncomfortable for me, and besides the person's behavior is not that bad."

You're rationalizing away what you need to do. You're avoiding what you know needs to be addressed because it's going to be hard on you to have that conversation. However, if you really care about this person and the good of the organization, you will have this uncomfortable conversation.

Being candid is an act of leadership and it's one of the harder acts of leadership, but it's also one of the more important.

CONDUCT A BUSINESS PHYSICAL

My client had just arrived back from his annual physical at the Cooper Clinic in Dallas. As a senior executive in this Fortune 50 Company, he was required to get a thorough physical every year. He told me how useful all of the information was because it helped him to understand what he was doing to remain healthy, what he was doing that was hurting his health, and what he could be doing to improve his health.

The very next topic we dove into was execution in his organization. He was responsible for about a $900 Million region. He was frustrated at the number of redundant and outdated processes his staff members were still using. He felt the organization was getting in its own way.

I looked at him, and said, "Why don't you combine those last two topics?"

He said, "What are you talking about?"

"Why don't you give your business a physical just like what they did for you at the Cooper Clinic?"

"I like that. We're going to do it."

For the next 45 days, he and his direct reports dove into the details of the processes being used throughout the organization. First, they made a list of every process being used in every department. Then they examined the processes and eliminated those that were redundant or so far outdated they had no relationship to the current business. Of the remaining processes, they asked themselves which ones were working effectively and which ones needed to be improved or eliminated. Then they worked to improve the processes they decided to focus on.

It took a lot of time and effort, but they significantly cleaned up the way people did their work and results improved significantly. It wasn't that his staff members weren't working hard. The problem was the system had been gummed up with too many processes in place.

Execution is accomplishing what has been planned. The key is to keep searching for ways to improve execution in your organization. This can range from process issues to people issues.

Innovate to Generate Sustainable Success

I define innovation as creating more appropriate value for other people and delivering it through a better experience for them. Notice once again the enormous importance of value and values. It's not just what you provide. It's also how you provide it. I used to say innovation was about creating greater value for other people that they would be willing to pay more for. However, as I will explain, this is a very limiting way of looking at innovation.

A PROCESS FOR INNOVATING

Coming up with innovative ideas is often looked at as unbridled, chaotic brainstorming that is totally fun. It might be fun to sit around and throw ideas out on the table, but it can be an incredibly inefficient use of time, energy, and dollars unless it is purposeful and channeled. I suggest you follow these three steps.

1. Clarify a customer objective.

2. Search for hotspots of too much value or too little value.

3. Iterate or eliminate.

Step #1: Clarify a Customer Objective

What does the customer want to achieve? Customers may not know what resource they want or need to achieve their desired objective, but they do have a pretty good idea of what they want to accomplish.

Answer this question: What does my customer, or my desired customer, want to accomplish? If you have spent time with your customer and invested time in understanding what is important to him or her, then this is not complicated to answer, but it does take a few minutes to clarify the answer and write it down. You may have to discuss this with other people in your organization to hone the answer.

For the sake of an example, let's say the person wants to travel from point A to point B, which is 50 miles away.

Step #2: Search for Hotspots of Too Much Value or Too Little Value

Value is anything that helps a person achieve what he or she wants to achieve. If the current solution is providing more value than the person needs to achieve what he or she wants, you have a great opportunity for innovation. If the current solution is not providing enough value for the person to achieve what he or she wants, you also have a great opportunity for innovation. I call these two scenarios "hot spots for innovation." A terrific book on this topic is *The Innovator's Solution* by Clayton Christensen.

Step two is to answer these questions: Where does the current solution provide the person with too much value? Where does the current solution provide the person with too little value?

Go back through history and reconsider the situation of wanting to travel 50 miles.

Walking was a solution, but it was of too little value. It took several days and was exhausting and you couldn't carry much. Riding a horse cost more money, but it provided a lot more appropriate value for going 50 miles. However, it was painful to ride on a horse all day so that provided another opportunity to innovate. A covered wagon was created, which allowed the person to sit down and carry more belongings on the trip. Yet, no matter how hard people tried, they could only get their horses to move at a certain pace. Trains provided more value because they moved a lot of people at much greater speeds than horse-drawn carriages. The problem was trains only went to specific places. If you wanted to go somewhere else, you were out of luck. Bicycles were an option for shorter distances, but they didn't provide enough value for a 50-mile trip. Then fancy automobiles were created and they allowed the driver to go in a variety of directions for much longer distances, but they were way too expensive for everyone except the absolute wealthiest people. They provided too much value, which left an opportunity to innovate by creating an automobile that provided more appropriate value. Henry Ford provided this innovation. Helicopters and small airplanes were invented, but they provided too much value for average consumers and therefore were not effective in replacing automobiles, except in very rare situations.

Two Case Studies of Finding Inappropriate Value

Here are two famous examples of companies who found situations where customers were receiving inappropriate value. The first is about people who were receiving too much value, and the second is about people who were receiving too little value.

McDonald's McCafe was a solution for people who wanted a great coffee product at a lower price than Starbuck's was offering. McDonald's recognized a situation where people wanted a certain level of coffee, but weren't willing or didn't want to pay the prices at Starbuck's. The Starbuck's prices were not appropriate for the level of value that certain customers were willing or wanting to pay for. Consequently, there was a huge opening for someone to step into and innovate, and McDonald's did it beautifully. They created great beverage products at reasonable prices, and their revenue soared.

People wanted to have their phone and music and internet access with them at all times so they were willing to carry their phone and music player and portable computer with them. Consequently, this was a hotspot for an innovative solution. The iPhone came along and provided much more appropriate value than carrying all three devices around. The original iPhone in 2007 cost a great deal more than the cell phones people had, but it provided much greater value for people, and Apple's revenue skyrocketed.

A Skill of Innovation

A key skill for an innovator to develop is to search for opportunities where too much value or too little value is currently being offered. Train yourself to put on your "value lenses" and leverage observations, conversations, and hands-on experiences to identify situations where your current customers, or desired customers, are receiving inappropriate value. A great book on this skill is *The Art of Innovation* by Tom Kelley of IDEO fame.

Don't do this all by yourself. Get together with other people from your business and discuss what they see in the marketplace in terms of where people receive more value than they need or less value than they need to achieve their objectives. It's not a good use of time to just come up with ideas for new products and services. You need a focused starting point.

Identify a customer objective. Then for every product or service these customers are currently purchasing to help them achieve this objective, ask yourself, "How is this product or service providing more value than the customer needs?" and "How is this product or service not providing enough value for this customer to achieve what he or she wants to achieve?"

If the current solution is providing too much value, is there a product or service that you can create that will provide more appropriate value at a lower price to the customer? In this case, price is the key differentiator. This is a remarkably effective way to break into a new market and compete with the established players in the industry. However, make sure you are not just delivering the same value as before and dropping the price. If you keep the value the same and lower your price, you are fighting a price war, and that is a surefire way to eventually ruin your business. The innovative approach is to create a product or service that delivers just the right amount of value for the customer to achieve his or her objective and lowers your cost in providing this product or service. Then you can legitimately offer it at a lower price to your customers without continually crushing your profit margins.

If the current solution is providing too little value for customers, then it's a waste of their money because the product or service doesn't help them achieve what they want. No matter how cheap it is, it's still a waste of money. In this case, a more valuable product or service is the key differentiator. Is there a product or service you can create to help the customer achieve the desired outcome? Don't worry if your product or service is priced higher than the competition. The key is for it to actually help the customer achieve what he or she wants.

Remember when the first iPod came out. It was October 2001, and the iPod costs $495 and held 1,000 songs. Critics said no one would spend that much money. They said iPod stood for "idiots price our devices." As my daughter, Sarah, says, "Ah, wrooooong." People were very willing to pay for greater value, just as they were in 2007 when the iPhone came out and in 2010 when the iPad came out. As you might recall the economy was very, very bad in October 2001 and in January 2010. However, people stepped up and paid for the greater value because it helped them to a much greater degree to achieve what they wanted.

Step #3: Iterate or Eliminate

Now you are ready to develop products and services that will create and deliver appropriate value for your desired customers. There are two approaches you can choose from. You can use either or both of them.

The first approach is to iterate. According to dictionary.com, iteration means a problem-solving method in which a succession of approximations, each building on the one preceding, is used to achieve a desired degree of accuracy. To iterate in your business take one of your existing products or services, or one of your competitor's existing products or services, and adjust it a little bit to provide more appropriate value for your customers. Of course, do not infringe on anybody's copyrights. When McDonald's got rid of their Salad Shakers and introduced their Premium Salads, it was an iteration. When Apple created the iPod Touch, it was an iteration.

The second approach is to eliminate. According to dictionary.com, eliminate means to remove from further consideration or competition. CDs (Compact Discs) eliminated the need for vinyl records, eReaders could eliminate the need for hard copy books, and cars eliminated the need for horse-drawn carriages. Is there a product or a service you can create that will eliminate the need for the current solution customers use to achieve their desired outcome?

The reason why Apple became one of the most valuable companies in the world and why McDonald's revitalized its brand and was named the best-managed company in the world by *Fortune* magazine in 2011 is because they combined iterations and eliminations for more than 10 years.

The iPod eliminated the need for the stereo system, iTunes eliminated the need to buy a cd, the iPhone eliminated the need for a cell phone and an iPod, the iPad eliminated the need for a textbook, and iCloud eliminated the need for a computer. The Redbox at McDonald's eliminated the need to go to Blockbuster and the McCafe eliminated the need to go Starbuck's. Notice one company is high-tech and the other is low-tech, and yet they both leveraged iterations and eliminations to drive better sustainable profitable growth.

Summarizing the Three Steps in The Process of Innovation

Focus intensely on these three steps to effectively innovate a new product or service: clarify a customer's objective, find hotspots of too much value or too little value for the customer in the current products and services, and iterate and/or eliminate in order to create more appropriate value for the customer and deliver it through a better experience for him or her.

The opportunities are there for the taking. As you begin to move your ideas into action, remember this mantra: Test small, improve, test again, improve…roll out. It might take you awhile to come out with an innovative new product or service, but if you follow these few steps I believe they will help you do so in a more efficient and effective manner.

OPTIMIZE THE CONDITIONS FOR GREAT INNOVATIONS

Without the ability to innovate an organization will eventually be left behind and will degenerate. This is true in every industry, every country, every for-profit organization, and every not-for-profit organization. The purpose of innovating is to help your organization achieve better sustainable success. You do that by consistently creating more appropriate value for other people and improving the experience those people go through in receiving that value.

In this section, I will explain a variety of the conditions that increase your chances for creating and delivering great innovations, the kind that really make a difference for your desired customers. At the end of each condition is a question to help you clarify whether or not you are meeting that condition.

Condition #1 for Innovating: Define the Parameters You
will Innovate Within

You can't do it all. I know this is an obvious thing to say, but when a business needs to deliver a good result every quarter sometimes the low-hanging fruit can look tempting, even though it's not at all related to what you want your business to focus on. Without realizing it, you can end up with people throughout your organization working on all kinds of things in the hopes of generating some short-term cash. The problem is that approach rarely creates meaningful innovations.

Even when he was painting the 12,000 square feet of ceiling space in the Sistine Chapel, Michelangelo knew he still had a defined space to work within. It was a big project, but it had parameters. Even when Apple expanded its strategy to focus on The Digital Lifestyle, it still had a defined area to work within. It didn't go off and build plastic toys for children or reinvent the assisted living industry.

By defining the boundaries for your innovations, you are also defining what you are not going to do. This is a critically important condition. Without it, you will be tempted to dive into every type of product or service you might be paid for. It would be like a kid wanting to earn extra spending money and so he sets up a lemonade stand for a week and then mows lawns for a week and then watches people's dogs for a week. It's hard to really become great at anything if you constantly change your focal point. It's hard work to not allow yourself to wander into different things. Focusing your attention on one thing helps you to be great at something rather than being mediocre at a lot of things.

What are the parameters you are going to innovate within?

Condition #2 for Innovating: Develop an Improvement Mindset

In my opinion, a great book is both simple and powerful. *Mindset* by Dr. Carol Dweck, a psychology professor at Stanford University, is an example of a great book. She focuses her attention on a simple concept: whether a person has a fixed mindset or a growth mindset will greatly impact his or her future behaviors.

She wrote, "The growth mindset is based on the belief that your basic qualities are things you can cultivate through your efforts…Believing that your qualities are carved in stone – the fixed mindset – creates an urgency to prove yourself over and over. If you have only a certain amount of intelligence, a certain personality, and a certain moral character – well, then you'd better prove you have a healthy dose of them. It simply wouldn't do to look or feel deficient in these most basic characteristics."

If you have a fixed mindset, you are unlikely to create a great innovation. Innovations are messy. They don't always look good. They require perseverance and an ability to know when to let go. If you believe every attempt you make is an opportunity to learn something that can improve a future attempt, you will likely hang in there when others might not. You will see each step as being valuable because it will help you to improve. If you have a fixed mindset, the messiness can feel overwhelming. You will feel that if what you know right now is all you are ever going to know than you might as well not embarrass yourself any further.

How can you get better at improving the innovation you are working on?

Condition #3 for Innovating: Know the Lone Genius is Pure Mythology

Here are two fairly common myths: Steve Jobs invented the first personal computer and Michelangelo painted the Sistine Chapel by himself while lying on his back. They sound good, but they aren't true. The Apple I was formalized by Steve Wozniak, but even his efforts were based on numerous conversations within The Homebrew Computer Club and fueled by the January 1975 issue of *Popular Mechanics* magazine. Michelangelo didn't lay on his back and he didn't paint the chapel by himself. He recruited a team of people to paint the chapel as a team project. He organized them into sections and outlined the work they needed to do. Parts of the project he painted by himself, but not all of it. If you're interested in what it took to create one of the greatest masterpieces ever made, I recommend you read *Michelangelo and the Pope's Chapel* by Ross King.

I facilitated a client meeting where eight senior executives debated the topic of whether a group of people are always smarter than any individual. Is it true that eight people discussing a topic will always come up with a better idea than a single person, or is it true that one individual can have a better idea than the eight people can come up with by bouncing their ideas around the table?

In the end, we landed on the idea that at any given moment any one of the individuals in the group might have a better idea than the whole group came up with, but we wouldn't know which person had the best idea unless we let each person share his or her insights. Sometimes a great idea is the synthesis of two ideas that were stated by different people in the group, and other times one person in the group will come up with the best idea. However, what is least likely to be true is the same person will always have the best idea in the group. This is the mythology of the lone genius. Don't allow yourself to fall into this category. I encourage you to read Chapter Five in the book, *The Art of Innovation*.

What insights are you gaining from other people?

Condition #4 for Innovating: Practice in a Deliberate Manner over a Long Period of Time

Here's one more salute to Anders Ericsson.

To develop a truly great innovation, you need to work at the details of the product or service for a very long time. You need to work to understand the needs of your customers better. You need to work to deliver the product or service in a way that is better for your customer. Look at your efforts in all of these areas as a series of practices or training sessions where each one is preparing you to become even better at creating a great innovation. Learn from every one of them and continually compile your ideas toward making something magnificent. Remember Anders Ericsson's emphasis on deliberate practice and the 10,000-Hour Rule from Chapter One.

How are you continually practicing the skills you need to create your desired innovation?

Condition #5 for Innovating: Avoid the Futility of Avoiding Failure

In 1995, the film, *Apollo 13*, first hit the big screen. Two phrases from the film have lived on: "Houston, we have a problem." and "Failure is not an option." In this story failure would have meant astronauts died and so the phrase made sense in this context. Since 1995 I have heard "failure is not an option" in countless meetings where people's lives were not at stake, but as so often happens a phrase from a film got embedded in society and we accepted it as the absolute truth.

Let me clarify. In business, failure is always an option. In your attempt to create more appropriate value for your customers and deliver it through a better experience for them, you might fail. People might not like it. They might not buy it. They might get angry and say bad things about your organization. If you're not okay with that, then you truly do have a problem, which is you are highly unlikely to ever create something of great value. Do your very best and then accept the response. Whether it's loved or hated, you can learn something from the experience and apply that something in the future to make an even better product or service.

Another great book (remember simple and powerful) is *The Innovator's Dilemma* by Clayton Christensen. He uses a variety of examples to show why highly successful companies tend to lose their momentum. In essence, they stop innovating. They don't want to risk sabotaging one of the successful products or services they developed in the past by developing a more innovative product or service in the future. Instead they let somebody else pass them by. In other words, they fail as an organization because they want to avoid failing.

Are you okay if your innovation is not successful? Are you okay if your new innovation wipes out your old innovation? If not, then you're going to have a problem.

Condition #6 for Innovating: Create a Crisis If You Need One

Crises can be wonderful things. They can stir successful companies to new heights of focus and attention and innovation. They can get people to work together who could barely speak to one another during good times. They can force people to make decisions and get on with the business of creating significantly better products and services.

Question: what do you do when you are not in a crisis? Answer: create one.

Create a crisis by hyping the importance of a deadline, by praising the competition and all they are doing to advance past your team, and by talking about the historic mark your organization can achieve and the legacy it will leave behind if only it would become more urgent. I'm not talking about beating people up or wearing them down. I'm talking about increasing the sense of urgency in the organization to continually become all that it is capable of being. Talk about how every day matters because it might be the day you develop a breakthrough idea for your customers.

It's nice to talk about putting action items in an "important, but not urgent" bucket. The problem is they tend to stay in that bucket. You need to create a sense of urgency in the absence of emergency. You have to believe you absolutely, positively need to focus today on finding some insight to improve your product or service or otherwise your whole organization might collapse. If your organization, your work group, your career, your family, and your life depended on you creating a product or service that delivered more appropriate value to your desired customers in a more effective way for them, would you get started today? You need to have that sense of urgency regarding innovations every day.

How can you increase your team's sense of urgency?

Condition #7 for Innovating: Be Willing to Stop and Start Over

Two of my favorite stories about Steve Jobs and Michelangelo are when they brought their innovations to a complete halt.

Steve Jobs bought Pixar Animation Studios in January 1986 and funded it for a period of 10 years with no profits. Zero. Zilch. Every quarter was a losing quarter. He, Ed Catmull, and John Lasseter had a dream of creating the first feature-length, computer-animated film, and the dream was costing Jobs a fortune. They named the film, *Toy Story*. However, after eight years of losing money it became painfully clear to John Lasseter and Steve Jobs the script needed to be rewritten. The characters needed to be friendlier. They stopped the film and started over with a new script. Jobs continued to pour his own money into the project even though it would now take two more years to complete.

Michelangelo was given a fixed amount of money to paint the Sistine Chapel. From that money he had to hire his assistants and purchase the paint, brushes, plaster, and scaffolding to complete the project. He began on May 10, 1508. After a great deal of effort in painting the scene called The Flood, he and his team members realized something was terribly wrong in January 1509 when they saw a fungus appear on their paintings. In the end, they realized they had put the plaster on the wall when it was too wet. Michelangelo realized that nothing great would be created if he continued on. Consequently, he ordered his employees to scrape the plaster off the wall and start all over again.

Great innovators have the guts to say, "We made a mistake. We need to stop and start over." How embarrassing and frustrating and costly that must have been for Steve Jobs and Michelangelo. Yet they did it over and over again. Near the launch of the original iPad, Jobs realized that he and the other team members had made a mistake. They needed the glass to go all the way to the edge. So they halted the project and redid the glass. The rest is history.

Are you willing to start your project over again when you realize there is a better path? If not, don't innovate.

Condition #8 for Innovating: Understand the Importance of Passion

In August 1990 I returned to the high school I attended to be an Algebra I teacher. My degree was in Mechanical Engineering and I had taken Calculus IV and Differential Equations. I had the technical knowledge to teach Algebra I, and I had an ability to explain ideas in a way other people could understand them. The problem was I had very little passion for math. I just didn't care about the Quadratic Equation. I didn't care to dig into the details of the subject to learn it better. I liked teaching and I liked the students, but I didn't care about my subject. Consequently, I never improved as a math teacher over the next seven and a half years.

I taught math exactly the same way on my last day as I did on my first day even though there had been significant advances in the graphing calculator during my tenure. I was competent, but I never improved. My passion was learning ideas on how people achieved great successes and sustained that level of performance for a long time. At every opportunity I went to the school library with a book in my hand about how individuals and organizations achieved great successes. I wrote down every good idea I could find in those books.

Sitting four feet away from me in the math department office was Tom Becvar, my former high school teacher, the chairman of the math department, and a true teacher extraordinaire. Tom taught the BC Calculus course. He had been a great teacher for 20 years when I arrived, but he still worked at understanding the details of all the problems before he taught them to his students. He went on to develop innovative ways to teach Calculus. He taught other high school teachers how to teach Calculus. He became a nationally respected advisor on the AP Calculus tests. He was named High School National Teacher of the Year by several organizations. Many adults today will say Tom Becvar is the greatest teacher they ever had. Tom was one of my mentors. He taught me a great deal about how to be a teacher.

What was the difference between us? I had taken math courses far beyond high school math. I could explain information well to other people. I liked being with the students. The difference was our passions. Tom loved math. I loved learning and teaching ideas on improving individual and organizational performance. In 1991 I created a week-long course for high school students called The Adventure of Life Course. It was about strengthening self-confidence and self-esteem. That course laid the groundwork for the business I eventually created in 1998. Ultimately, our passions took us down two different paths.

To be a great innovator, you have to truly care about the products and services you are creating. You have to be over-the-top passionate about the value you are creating for other people. If you don't passionately care about what you are doing, how can you possibly expect your customers to care?

In 1997, upon his return to Apple, Steve Jobs said, "Marketing is about values. Apple at its core value believes that people with passion can change the world for the better." His passion and the passion of other people at Apple had always been to democratize great electronic technology. He wanted to put simple, great tools in the hands of as many people as possible to help them do what they were passionate about.

I attended a meeting at Anheuser-Busch InBev as a consultant where senior-level engineers stood together with passion as they studied how the lids were sealed on precisely to the cans in order to maintain the quality of the beer. I've been at McDonald's meetings where McDonald's corporate staff members and owner/operators studied intensely the exact positioning of a fry station so it would optimize the speed with which customers were served. I've sat in Toyota Financial Services meetings where Finance & Insurance Managers would huddle together to figure out the simplest way for the customers to understand the details of a leasing or loan agreement. I have facilitated meetings with Marriott employees where they were engaged in intense conversations about how to provide more effective leadership for their associates.

Great companies have people who care about the value they are creating for other people. They get emotional over the details. They have a Tom Becvar-like passion for what they do and how they can do it better.

Do you really care about the product or service you are creating for other people? If not, is there someone else in your organization who is passionate about this project? If not, don't go after this innovation.

Summary of the Conditions for Great Innovations

Innovating sounds so sexy and glamorous. It sounds refreshing and exciting. The reality is innovating is work, really, really hard work. You have to be passionate and purposeful and committed. You have to look at every setback as a learning experience, not as a defining moment. You have to persevere beyond anything you used to think was reasonable. You have to observe people for a ridiculous amount of time until you really understand what they truly need. However, in the end innovating is how you will make your organization and the world a better place. This is why it is worth it.

APPLY THE VALUE FORMULA EVERY DAY

In giving a speech at Boeing, I shared my definition of value. I said, "Value is anything that increases the chances the other person will achieve what he or she wants to achieve." An audience member asked me, "How do you measure value?" That stumped me. I realized right away my definition was insufficient. Something could be of little value or great value to another person, but my definition wouldn't be able to differentiate between the two.

Then I thought about my years of working with executives at McDonald's. I always admired the way McDonald's people worked to make every part of their business processes simpler and simpler. I recalled their simple formula for value to a customer. It read: $V = QSC/P$.

For McDonald's, value to the customer is equal to the quality of the product times fast, accurate, and friendly service times the cleanliness of the restaurant divided by the price of the transaction. I watched many times as executives at McDonald's used that formula to determine what future products and services to provide to customers. I loved how it made the conversations so much more practical than they otherwise would have been.

As much as I liked their formula, I needed something simpler and more universal that could be applied to every business regardless of the industry. I landed on the following Value Formula: $V = I/C$.

Value to the customer equals the improvement in his or her desired outcome divided by his or her cost of achieving that improvement. Cost to the customer includes his or her investment of money, time, and energy.

Questions Derived from The Value Formula

There is nothing remotely complicated or new about this formula. However, like jogging and doing pushups, the power is not in its complexity, but rather in us actually using it every day.

Here are three Value Formula Questions for you to think about in your business.

What outcome does your customer want to improve?

How can your organization do better at helping this customer improve his or her achievement of this outcome?

How can your organization reduce the amount of money, time, and/or energy the person has to invest in order to achieve this improvement in his or her desired outcome?

Many times I have heard executives talk about massive transformational efforts to improve their organization's brand, innovations, leadership, and talent management. Rather than launching into a long-term, highly expensive, and intensely complicated commitment, I encourage you to gather a group of key decision makers within your company and just discuss their answers to these three Value Formula Questions. The answers will largely determine your brand, your innovations, the types of people you hire and develop, and the tactics you want to influence your employees toward accomplishing.

Apply The Value Formula Looking Backward

Look at past examples where products changed because of the increased value for the customer. Take the shift in the 1980s from vinyl records to compact discs. Assume for the moment the price stayed the same for an album on a vinyl record and a compact disc.

First, look at the top half, the "I" in The Value Formula. Customers wanted to be able to hear their favorite songs throughout the day. The compact disc was much more mobile than the vinyl record. You couldn't very well carry a turntable around with you, but you could have a compact disc player with you at all times.

Now, look at the bottom half, the "C" of the Value Formula. The price wasn't reduced, but there was a savings in terms of the cost of storing compact discs versus vinyl records. It was a lot easier to store them and to carry them around.

By improving the "I" and lowering the "C" the "V" went way, way up. Consequently, compact discs replaced vinyl records almost overnight.

Apply The Value Formula Looking Forward

You can apply this same mindset to any industry. First, identify the customer's desired outcome, and then work to improve this outcome while simultaneously reducing the cost in terms of money, time, and/or energy on the part of the customer.

Consider the residential real estate market. Customers want their ideal home in their ideal community. Anything that can be done to improve the customer's result within this desired objective will improve the "I" in the formula, and anything that can be done to reduce the customer's investment of money, time, and/or energy to find their ideal home in their ideal community will lower the "C".

Look at The Value Formula through the Perspective of Two Very Valuable Companies

Exxon Mobil helps customers have the freedom to travel in their own cars wherever they want to go that is within driving distance. By constantly searching for and refining oil, they provide the fuel for freedom. As they make the gasoline higher quality and work to reduce its price, they are reducing the cost in terms of money, time, and energy for people to maintain the freedom they want in their lives. Sometimes people complain about the cost of a gallon of gasoline, but they don't very often look at the improvement that gallon of gasoline brings to their lives in terms of increased freedom and independence.

Through its constant commitment to innovation, Apple produced a mind-boggling 27" iMac desktop computer with 32 GB of memory that sold for $1800 in 2013. In 1984, a guy down the hall from me in my college dorm bought the original Macintosh personal computer with 128 kB of memory for $2,500. Now think about The Value Formula. Customers want to be able to do their creative work fast and store it in reliable ways. Think about how Apple dramatically increased the "I" while equally dramatically reducing the "C" in just the one example of a desktop computer in those 30 years. Not only did this computer become much, much less expensive in dollars, especially when you factor in the inflation over those three decades, but it also cost a great deal less in terms of reduced time and energy wasted because the computer didn't freeze up or run into errors anywhere near as often.

Business Strategy Happens at the Intersection of Value

When you make a business investment, there are actually two ways to look at value. First, what will increase value for your customers? Second, what will increase value for your company? Both perspectives need to be taken into consideration as you determine your strategy for moving forward. Look at The Value Formula from the perspective of your business and answer these questions.

What are your desired business outcomes?

What can you do better to improve the achievement of those desired outcomes?

What are you willing to invest in terms of money, time, and energy in order to try to achieve those desired improvements for your business?

That last question is the critical parameter you have to keep in mind as you determine your strategy for the immediate and long-term future. The good news is this parameter can keep you from ruining your business.

In his book, *The Strategy Paradox: why committing to success leads to failure (and what to do about it)*, Michael Raynor makes the point over and over that the primary reason for businesses succeeding is also the primary reason for businesses failing. He explains that going all out to support a long-term committed strategy can produce spectacular successes for a business as well as the collapse of the business.

In order to thrive as a business, you first have to survive as a business. This means you have to apply The Value Formula from your business's perspective as well as for the customer. If you go all out to create greater value for your customer with the hopes of improving your desired business outcomes while ignoring the cost to your business, you may very well destroy your business.

Consider the cost to your organization in terms of money, time, and energy to produce the improved value for your customer and decide if your organization can realistically handle that cost before moving into action. If it cannot, then be willing to reduce the improvement in your desired outcomes so you can survive as an organization and still improve the value to the customer, even though it might be to a lesser degree than you wanted. Apple didn't build the iMac, iPod, iPhone, and iPad in one summer. They did what they could do a little at a time.

It is important to measure the value you produce both for your customers and your organization. You do want to improve the desired outcomes for both while working to reduce the cost for both in terms of money, time, and energy invested. Keep The Value Formula at the center of your decision making each day.

WORKING IN THE CREATIVITY AGE

When I was a kid, there was a very popular song on the radio called, *The Age of Aquarius*. It was written in 1969. The lyrics included these words: "This is the dawning of the Age of Aquarius. Harmony and under-standing, sympathy and trust abounding, no more falsehoods or derisions, golden living, dreams of visions."

That age never quite happened, but right now we are living in an age that really is happening. It's called the Creativity Age. The world has evolved from the Stone Age to the Agricultural Age to the Industrial Age to the Information Age to the Creativity Age. This era is relatively new. It began with the internet and has gained speed ever since with technologies connecting people all over the world and giving them opportunities to do things they could never have done before.

The Creativity Age has caused massive upheaval for many organiza-tions and individuals and shut down many businesses. It certainly upended many people's otherwise wonderful careers. It cut across national borders, shrunk the planet, and changed how organizations and individuals inter-acted with each other. It also created enormous opportunities for people all over the world, and the crazy thing is its impact is only going to get bigger and bigger. The Creativity Age is here to stay.

Where Paid Work Happens

If you're going to earn a paycheck, it's going to happen in one of a few ways. You will either work for a for-profit or a not-for-profit organization. You will either own a business or work for someone else. You will either manage the efforts of other people or you will not. You will either work with other people in an organization or you will work completely by your-self. Your work today and in the future is going to fall into one or more of those categories.

Toss out your title and your industry and the size of your organization and your bonus and where you went to school. None of that stuff really matters. Regardless of the way in which you work, there are certain key elements that absolutely matter in the Creativity Age. Here are five of the most important.

Add Value

Value is anything that increases the chances the other person will achieve what he or she wants to achieve. Regardless of your title or your income or the size of your organization or your industry, you have one critically important job to do today. That job is to add value. Every day you have to ask yourself, "Today how am I going to create value for other people and deliver it as well as I can?" This is not a fun little saying to post on your wall and smile about. You have to have a committed drive to creating and delivering value every day. This is the one and only way to survive and thrive in the Creativity Age.

The job of today is not the heavy lifting of the 1800s or the gathering of information of the 1970s. The main job is to create value and deliver it to other people. You might be creating and delivering value to your team members who are part of a huge organizational effort. You might be on the front line with your customers. You might be running a training ses-sion or deciding who to hire or serving as an engineer on a new product development or working in a not-for-profit organization focused on deliv-ering food to the needy or teaching elementary school kids or deciding on the strategic direction of a Fortune 100 company. It doesn't matter what your role is or where you work. What does matter, and it matters a lot, is that you step back from your activities and ask yourself, "What can I do or make that would be of appropriate value for other people, and how can I deliver this value to them?"

If you are unemployed or are looking to work at a different organiza-tion, answer the same question. What can you do to create and deliver value for a new organization? Be very, very clear in your mind about your answer so you can clearly communicate it to other people.

Observe, Listen, Read, and Combine

The old saying, "There is nothing new under the sun" is true, but only tells part of the story. The creative person looks to create new value by observing other people, listening to their thoughts, reading their stories, and combining the ideas into new products and services. The great advantage of today is you can "observe" a great deal of what is happening anywhere in the world via the internet, you can listen to a great deal of what people have to say from anywhere in the world via Google.com, you can read any book or magazine in an instant on an iPad or Kindle or Nook or Galaxy Tablet, and you can combine an incredible array of products and services and ideas that already exist into something new and valuable for other people. These four skills make up the generator of creativity. They're free. Use them every day.

Care Immensely about What You Do

After having lunch with my mom one day, I drove her back to her condominium and we paused in the parking lot. She pointed to a group of men who had raked and swept a giant pile of leaves together. They were putting the leaves into a giant mulching machine. She said, "Those men care about their work. Look how clean the parking lots are. I'm going to go tell them what a great job they are doing."

In the Creativity Age every detail matters a lot. Regardless of where you live, you are competing with other talented people all over the world. No country has an insurmountable advantage over another. It's an open game of competition. Consequently, the key is to create and deliver as much value as you can every day. Ultimately, it comes down to caring enormously about what you do.

Where can you learn to care this much?

Think about your family members, your best friends, and other people you love dearly. Describe how you care about them. Write it down. Then apply that level of caring to the work you do every day.

Go to a place you admire: a restaurant, a store, a barbershop or beauty salon, or a favorite vacation destination. Study how the people who work there care about their customers. Write down what you see. Fix in your mind how you will apply some of those approaches in your work.

Tomorrow at work care more than you have ever cared before. Take "caring about the details of your work" to a higher level than you have ever done. Then when you go in to work the day after tomorrow care more than you did the day before. Don't obsess over your bonus or your title. Just care about everything you do and you will find yourself doing it as well as you possibly can.

Connect to a Purpose

The people I know who are riveted with a purpose in their professional lives are the ones who care the most about every detail. They see their work as merely the mechanism for fulfilling a greatly engrained purpose. You have to know why you do what you do. There are only three great sources of passion that I know of. You either have to love what you do, love who you do it for, or both.

Some people love the work they do. They love building teams or they love making something that no one thought was possible or they love some aspect of their work. Some people don't love what they do, but they love who they do it for. They are helping to send a child to college or helping a child who has been mentally or physically challenged or being there for an aging parent. They love the person so much they are driven to do their best work every day. Some people both love the work they do and who they do it for. That's the formula for an even deeper sense of purpose at work and even greater creativity.

Fit within a Larger Picture

In the Creativity Age no one works in a silo. We are all connected to other people in our work. Even if you run a one-person business, your efforts are still interlinked with the work of other people. How does the value you create and deliver today fit within the larger picture of your organization, your community, or the world's marketplace? Working hard on the details of a project is only of real value if it helps other people to achieve what they want to achieve.

Those are five of the crucial keys for working successfully in the Creativity Age. In many ways, these are the same keys to a successful career that were true in earlier ages. However, back in those days you could count on getting a job in an organization and keeping it for the rest of your career. You could count on competition being mainly limited to your geographical area. Those parameters no longer exist. Now more than ever before you have to constantly be creative in finding ways to add more appropriate value to other people.

THE ADVANTAGES OF DISADVANTAGES

Many great achievements can be traced back to overcoming disadvantages. Many great failures can be traced back to a lack of disadvantages.

Be careful in complaining about your disadvantages and assuming your advantages will guarantee you success in life. Disadvantages can help you see your situation from different perspectives and find approaches to succeed you might not otherwise have found. Advantages can blind you from the necessity to keep searching for better ways to pursue success.

Challenges Propel Great Performances

In the 1770's people living in the American colonies had several disadvantages. They were excessively taxed, had virtually no representative voice in how they were being treated, and had almost a non-existent military to protect them from the British military. They lost battle after battle in the Revolutionary War. However, their disadvantages forced them to focus on what they could do. When the British military attacked them in America, they kept running away. The size of their country and their commitment to outlast the British became two of their greatest advantages. Eventually the British got tired of spending money and hurting their own men while chasing the Americans in a land so far away from their homeland. When the early Americans were piecing together their form of government, the last thing they wanted was to be under the rule of a small handful of people so they created something truly revolutionary: representative government. This form of governing a nation has spread around the world in the past couple of hundred years.

When Ralph Lauren started his business in 1967 he had certain disadvantages to overcome. He had no money, no store, no name recognition, no experience, and one client. Bloomingdale's agreed to sell his ties. However, these disadvantages allowed him to steadily focus on one part of his business at a time, namely in 1968 his first full line of Ralph Lauren menswear, in 1969 his first Polo Ralph Lauren store, in 1971 his first full Ralph Lauren womenswear line, in 1972 his first Ralph Lauren Polo shirt, and in 1978 his first Ralph Lauren fragrance.

If he had unlimited resources and scores of stores asking for his products when he first started, he may have never created each piece of his business with such care and attention to detail. If he had tons of money to spend and stores to fill up with products, he might have moved so fast he would have choked on his advantages.

Your Story of Overcoming Disadvantages and Challenges

The list of people converting disadvantages into great successes is endless and inspiring. Now turn toward yourself. Write down one great success you've had in your lifetime. Then write down the disadvantages or challenges you had to overcome to achieve this success. Then identify how those disadvantages forced you to look at your situation differently and ultimately helped you achieve success. Here are three questions to help you reach back into your vault of important memories and recall how you overcame disadvantages in the past.

1. What is one great success you've had in your lifetime?

2. What disadvantages or challenges did you have to overcome in order to achieve your success?

3. How did those disadvantages or challenges help you to find an alternative approach to achieve success?

Your Next Story of Overcoming Disadvantages and Challenges

Now I want you to focus on the present. There are massive challenges being faced by every business in the world right now. Take the time to answer these three questions.

1. What disadvantages or challenges is your business facing right now?

2. What alternative approaches to achieving success are those disadvantages and challenges forcing you to consider?

3. Specifically, what will you do to convert your disadvantages into advantages?

The absolute key here is to see that your disadvantages and challenges may very well be guiding you to extraordinary success. The essential attitude is to stay open to where you are being guided rather than getting mired down in complaining about the obstacles standing in the way of your current approach.

When I started my business leadership consulting firm in January 1998 I had a variety of disadvantages, which I am now very grateful for. I had no business background. My degree was in engineering and my previous jobs were as a college soccer coach and high school math teacher. Therefore, I had no business industry experience. I couldn't build my business by being an "industry expert." I had virtually no business connections, except for those business people my high school students were related to or my friends and family knew of. I met my first CEO client at a wedding where Barb was a bridesmaid. There was no one to pave the way for me through a series of clients. I did not overcome a personal tragedy, win a Super Bowl, or write a best-selling book. I had not been on a television show or in a movie.

These "disadvantages" forced me to think about how I was going to get work. Since I had no industry experience, I was forced to be open to working with people at companies from all kinds of different industries. I've now worked with clients in over 40 different industries. My cross-industry experience has become an asset for my business. Since I was not well known and had no compelling personal story of triumph to share, I had to focus on developing very practical ideas people could use right away to improve their performance and results.

My challenges forced me to read and read and read and to observe business managers and executives for thousands of hours in the flow of their daily business lives in order to understand what made some business people successful and others very unsuccessful. After I had spent 10 years primarily as an Executive Coach, my biggest client said they were no longer going to use any outside coaches. This guided me to focus even more on keynote speaking and seminars and writing. Since I had no amazing personal stories of overcoming tragedies or winning the World Series, I focused on teaching my ideas through ordinary everyday stories people could easily relate to.

As I look to the future, I'm focused not only on the advantages I've developed, but much more so on understanding what my current disadvantages and challenges are guiding me to consider as an alternative approach to achieving my objectives.

I very much encourage you to write down all of the disadvantages and challenges you are facing right now. Then work to identify what advantages those disadvantages are forcing you to uncover. If you feel everything is perfect, I want you to set for yourself a compelling challenge that will cause you to have to overcome certain obstacles. It's unhealthy for your business to think you have the world by the tail and have nothing to overcome. This can actually lead you on a path to failure because you may very well stop looking for innovative ways to achieve success.

INNOVATE ON A TIGHT BUDGET

A business innovation is the process of creating more appropriate value for your customers that they will pay for at a profit for your business. Your innovations have to do both: create more appropriate value for customers and ultimately increase the profit your organization makes. Creating value that erodes profit is not a business innovation. It's actually a self-induced death blow to your business. Here are seven ideas to consider when you are innovating on a tight budget.

Focus, Don't Spend

For many years I worked with executives in one of the world's largest companies. Each quarter we would study the business results of the industry in a wide variety of categories. Every quarter one of my client's competitors, which was much smaller and had far fewer resources than my client's organization, would win in several key performance categories. The employees at my client's organization worked incredibly hard on a large number of projects to create and deliver more value to the customers. They invested enormous resources in these innovative projects, and yet this small competitor kept outperforming them quarter after quarter.

Then one day my client hired one of the key executives from this competitor. On her second week on the job I asked her, "How in the world did your former company keep outperforming your new company?" What she said I will never forget.

"We had very, very limited resources. We couldn't try a lot of things. We had to succeed with the few projects we could afford to do. We were forced to concentrate on delivering great value on one thing at a time. Here we have tons of resources. That's the problem. It allows us to not have to focus in order to survive. So we end up doing too many projects and overwhelming our front-line employees and customers."

Within a few years my client's organization was achieving incredible results that were lasting far longer than ever before. What was the difference? In spite of having massive resources to work with my client's organization narrowed their focus to a few key areas. No longer did they allow themselves to go off on three dozen wild tangents. They poured all of their effort and concentration into improving just those few areas. They went on to achieve truly remarkable results quarter after quarter for more than a decade.

Note: recessions are good for innovation. It forces every company to operate within a tight budget and be extremely focused. This tight area of concentration generates far more useful innovations than the conceptual free-for-all companies often use during good economic times.

In one six-month stretch during the Great Recession of 2009, I served as a business speaker to the National Automobile Dealers Association, the National Association of Home Builders, and a national conference of a major residential real estate company. These were three of the hardest hit industries during this time. I didn't hear talk about gloom and doom at any of the meetings. I heard a lot of ideas about how people were working to create greater practical value for their customers in a few concentrated areas. It was clear everyone understood that innovative thinking was a requirement to survive through the recession and thrive on the other side of it.

What is the one area you are going to focus on improving for your customers?

Ask

Of course one way to find out the best area to focus on for customers is to ask the customers. I suggest a simple question such as, "If there was one thing about your experience with this product (or service) you would like improved, what would it be?"

Be patient. Customers don't have the answer on the tip of their tongues. Allow them to think. If they can't think of anything, you can follow up with probing questions on specific aspects of the product or service. Another approach is to ask, "What was of value to you with this product, what was not of value to you, and what would have been of greater value to you?"

Before you start to come up with an innovative product or service, ask your team a question you are trying to find the answer to. Say you want to create a new countertop in public bathrooms for the sinks and faucets. Your question might be, "How can we create a countertop that stays dry so a person can place a book or small bag on the countertop and the item won't get all wet while she washes her hands?"

Innovations don't have to be about computers or cell phones or medicine. Innovation is about creating more appropriate value for other people. This can happen in any industry.

See

Remember this: insight comes from sight. If you want to understand the customer experience in order to improve it, go see for yourself what it is customers go through. Don't just ask them for ideas on how to improve the experience. Go look for yourself.

One year I was in charge of the annual Valentine's Day Party for my social group at church, and so I ordered a quarter sheet cake for the party. A few hours before the event I went to the bakery, and asked the baker if I could see the cake before I paid for it. She opened the box, and it said, "Happy Valentine's Day, St. Lucas Women in Red". I looked at the cake, I looked at the baker, and I said, "Why does it say, 'St. Lucas Women in Red'?"

She pulled out the order form, and said, "It says right here, 'St. Lucas Women in Red.'"

I looked at it, and I said, "I meant I wanted the frosting in red, not the words 'in red.'"

She said, "No problem." She scooped off the red letters and replaced them with white frosting.

At the party I told this story. Someone else said, "I had the same experience at that bakery." If the manager of the bakery had been a customer of the bakery, then he or she may have gained the insight necessary to create a better experience for customers.

Stop and Start Over

Sometimes you have to start over from scratch. Don't feel compelled to merely tweak what you've always done. Don't be married to your current way of doing things. Once you've gained insights into what customers really want be willing to take out a blank sheet of paper and start with new ideas on what will deliver the value you want delivered to them.

Improve

A prototype is a model that represents what your idea will look like when it's put into action. You can create simple prototypes for both products and services. Use cheap, basic materials to assemble your prototype. Paper, napkins, paper towels, paper clips, cardboard, and Styrofoam work great. Don't use expensive materials to make fancy looking models. That's a waste of money.

When you explain your concept you can refer to the prototype and this may very well help the other person understand better what it is you're trying to get across. My favorite quote from the book, *The Art of Innovation*, is, "If a picture is worth a thousand words, then a prototype is worth a thousand pictures."

Start by having people in your group create five or six prototypes for the area of focus you're trying to improve. Have your group study the prototypes, capture the best ideas, and continue to make new prototypes as better ideas evolve.

Notice so far you have not spent very much money. You've invested time in talking with customers, observing customers, and developing prototypes. The process of innovation is not expensive. The primary investment is a mental investment, not a financial one.

Keep improving the prototypes until you land on the one you are ready to actually create and deliver into the marketplace. This is where the costs primarily occur. You will have to spend some money in producing the product or training people on the new service they will be delivering and on marketing the new product or service. Notice if you hold off on the spending until this stage you are able to provide something into the marketplace that has a far better chance of success at a lower overall investment from your business.

Sell

At some point you have to attempt to sell your innovation. You can't innovate in a vacuum forever. You've got to put your idea out in the marketplace and see how people respond to it. Innovation does not end with the first sale. Innovation is an on-going process. Find out what customers like and don't like in your new product or service, and keep working to make it more and more appropriate for them.

Find What Resonated With Customers

One important question to ask after your product or service has been in the market for a reasonable amount of time is, "Do customers feel they received the value we intended to deliver to them?"

There are benefits to you regardless of the answer to that question. If customers feel they are receiving the value you wanted to deliver, then you can tell how much this value is worth to them. If customers believe they are receiving some other value that was unintended, then find out what it is. Perhaps this unintended value can lead to great profits for your business. If customers feel they are receiving no value from this new product or service, then you can work to determine if you need to scratch the idea or merely modify it.

My point is don't just stop after you've sent the new product or service into the marketplace. Allow customers to teach you what you don't know about this new innovation. It doesn't matter what value you think you put into the marketplace. What does matter is what value your customers think you put into the marketplace.

Keep searching for, creating, and delivering more appropriate value for your customers. It is the key to surviving in tough times and thriving in good times.

ACCELERATE AND SUSTAIN EXCELLENCE

Since the word "excellence" means a lot of different things to different people, I'm going to start with my definition of excellence just so we're working off of the same page. To me, excellence means doing an activity as well as you can do it while searching for ways to do it better in the future. Consequently, excellence can be achieved at any point in your life. It's in your hands. If you are doing an activity as well as you can do it and you are looking for ways to do it better the next time, you are achieving excellence. Here are habits on how to sustain excellence over the long term.

Habit of Excellence #1: Be Ready For Your Moment

My senior year in high school I was in a play. It was the only play I was ever in. I had four lines to say, two in the first act and two in the second act. In the first act I delivered my two lines very well. I then had 45 minutes before my next scene. I stood behind the curtain and watched part of the play, I talked with the other actors and actresses, and then I went into the restroom to check my hat. I had to wear this big brown hat, and I wanted to make sure it looked okay.

Then with what I thought was about 10 minutes before my next scene I went behind the curtain to relax for a moment. In that instant the lead actress saw me, and yelled, "Coughlin, you are on right now!!!" And she pushed me from behind the curtain onto the stage. Without even looking up, I said my two lines as fast as I could and then went over and sat down on the chair where I was supposed to go in the scene. For the rest of scene I sat there sweating profusely. I had almost ruined the play for everyone else because I was not ready for my moment. I wasn't alert and prepared. Truth be told, I was lucky the lead actress saw me when she did.

To achieve excellence and to do the best you are capable of doing in whatever you are doing you have to be ready for your moment. You have to be prepared, and you have to be alert.

Habit of Excellence #2: Don't Compare Yourself to Other People, Learn From Them

Comparing yourself to other people is an absolute waste of time and energy.

It eats up time and energy you could be using to get better at what you are doing. You will always be able to find people who got lower grades than you, who are less popular than you, who are less athletic and less theatrical and less committed to the community than you, who have less stellar careers than you, who make less money than you do, and who live in a smaller house than you do.

However, if finding these people is what you have to do to feel good about yourself, then I have really bad news for you. You will also always be able to find people who got better grades than you, who are more popular than you, who are more athletic and more theatrical and more committed to the community than you, who have more stellar careers than you, who make more money than you, and who live in a bigger house than you.

Comparing yourself to others will absolutely drive you batty over time and keep you from ever achieving excellence.

Instead of comparing yourself to others, learn from other people. Learn from people you admire and from people you can't stand being around. Ask yourself, "What does this person do well that I might be able to use myself?" and "What does this person do that really turns me off, and how can I make sure I don't do it?" If you learn something from one other person every week, you will assemble an incredible toolbox for achieving excellence.

Habit of Excellence #3: Perform with Precision

In whatever you are doing, pay attention to the details and do each detail as well as you can. Don't try to do five things at once. Focus your attention on the one activity you are doing. Do that activity as well as you can and search for ways to do it better the next time. Stay focused.

Habit of Excellence #4: Have Fun

Drudgery is not a formula for excellence. If you hate every minute of doing a certain thing, you will never do it as well as you can do it. Have fun. Enjoy it. Turn it into a game. Don't be consumed with the result. Focus on the doing of the activity. Pretend you're a detective, and you are searching for clues on how to do it better.

Habit of Excellence #5: Do it as a Team Member

Excellence in a vacuum isn't much fun either. Look for opportunities to be a part of something bigger than just yourself. If your total focus is you, you are going to have a pretty boring life, one that is not going to generate excellence over the long term.

Look for ways to contribute your excellence to a cause you believe in. Honing your skills while volunteering for a meaningful cause can have multiple benefits. To improve your skills, they need to be applied toward something you really believe in. As you're working toward improving yourself imagine what you can do with this increased talent. Talent is the capacity to add value to other people. What will you do with your talent to help others today, tomorrow, and 20 years from now?

Habit of Excellence #6: Don't Let Anyone Talk You Out of Achieving Your Dreams

Life is funny. When you're in high school, everyone asks you, "What are you going to do with your life when you grow up?" People want you to dream big dreams. They want you to reach for the sky. Then you grow up and start to pursue those wild dreams, and people say, "When are you going to get serious and get a real job and make real money so you can raise kids to go after their dreams?"

If you don't go after your dreams, why should your kids go after theirs?

If you believe in a dream, go after it. Find something you really believe in and work toward achieving it. Not every dream will be realized and that's okay, but don't let someone else talk you out of achieving what you want to pursue. If you maintain the habit of going after your dreams, there's a chance you will do it for the rest of your life.

Habit of Excellence #7: Avoid Arrogance

The one guaranteed way to never achieve excellence is to be arrogant. Arrogance means you believe you already have all of the answers. I'm continually stunned by the number of mediocre performers who believe they have already learned all there is to know. I'm equally inspired by the amazing performers who keep working to get better every single day.

Again, excellence means doing something as well as you can do it while searching for ways to do it better in the future. If you do that over and over and over throughout your lifetime, you will develop the habit of excellence.

Feed Your Brand Every Day

Your organization's brand is the value customers think they receive when they buy your products and services. It is also the value prospective customers think they will receive if they do buy your products and services.

Every organization has a brand. It might be strong or weak, but it still exists. You don't own your brand. Your organization's brand exists outside of your business and inside the minds of your customers and your potential customers. You can't control what other people think about your organization and its products and services. The best you can do is try to strengthen the value you want your organization to be known for delivering.

The Financial Value of Your Brand

Sales are important. You have to make sales in the short term and over the long term in order to pay your bills, compensate your employees, and make a profit so you can stay in business. Selling is the lifeblood of every business. However, if all you do is focus on selling, you may end up with a very weak brand as an organization.

Think about the long-term financial strength in having a great brand like McDonald's, Coca-Cola, Google, Apple, Toyota, Marriott, Anheuser-Busch InBev, RE/MAX, and Disney. When your organization has a very weak brand in the marketplace, it makes the act of selling exponentially more difficult. When your organization has a very strong brand in the marketplace, it makes selling exponentially easier. The key to driving large numbers of sales is having a strong brand. A strong brand acts like a giant magnet where customers want to buy from you rather than you having to search far and wide to find a potential customer you then have to convince to buy from you.

Think of selling a Carrie Underwood song before she won American Idol and after she won American Idol. Compare selling a ticket to a Los

Angeles Galaxy soccer game before David Beckham showed up with selling a ticket while he played there. Compare selling hamburgers at a startup local restaurant with selling hamburgers at McDonald's. It's much easier to sell to them if people already believe you offer great value.

GAIN AND MAINTAIN A COMPETITIVE ADVANTAGE THAT MATTERS DEEPLY TO CUSTOMERS

The ultimate impact of a great business leader is to help his or her organization gain and maintain a competitive advantage that matters deeply to customers and allows it to generate sustainable profitable growth. This is the fruition of great leadership, teamwork, execution, innovation and branding.

Define and Own a Performance Category

For your organization to gain and maintain a competitive advantage, it has to be very clear which performance category your organization is competing in. Then your organization has to constantly improve the delivery of relevant value to customers within that narrow scope. Wal-Mart gained a competitive advantage in low-cost consumer goods and has maintained this advantage for many years. McDonald's gained an advantage in quick-service restaurants and has worked to maintain this advantage for several decades. Marriott gained an advantage in hospitality in the lodging market and has worked to sustain this advantage for over half a century.

A performance category is any description of a desired outcome for a customer. People carry lots of these in their mind at any given moment. Here are some:

Great family restaurant at reasonable prices within 10 minutes of my home.

Newest adult romantic comedy.

Best place to get my car taken care of.

Resort getaway that allows my spouse and I to relax and have fun.

For every one of these performance categories, and a whole lot more, customers and potential customers carry around one or at most two options in their mind. People almost always choose from their top two options for every performance category, and they choose their first option way more than the second. If your organization is not in the top two in your desired customer's mind for the performance category you want to compete in, you have virtually zero chance of building a great brand and generating sustainable profitable growth. Two excellent books on this topic are *Positioning* by Al Ries and Jack Trout and *The Dip* by Seth Godin.

The good news is you get to define the performance category you want to compete in. The key is this performance category has to matter enough to people that they are willing to pay for the products and services of whatever organization is their top choice. Ultimately, you want to gain and maintain a competitive advantage over every other organization in this performance category.

Why You?

To increase your understanding of what performance category your organization is competing in, write down why your current customers buy from your organization. Take your time and think about every reason why someone buys from your organization. Write down all of these reasons. Involve other executives and managers and front-line employees and customers to hear their opinions on this topic. It's a very important one.

After you read through all of the statements, fill in the blank in either of these two statements:

We are in the business of _____ .

We are in the _____ business.

After you determine the business you're in, which is the performance category you are competing in, make sure everything you do supports what you want to be known for. The key is to gain and maintain a competitive advantage over other organizations that want to compete in this category so you are always either the first or the second choice for a significant number of customers in this category. This essentially becomes your branding effort.

Continually Strengthen your Business Wagon Wheel

The covered wagon was critical to the success of America. In the mid-1800s, thousands of families put all of their belongings into covered wagons and moved themselves and their belongings across the Great Plains to Oregon and California. The most important part of the covered wagon was the wagon wheel. The wagon wheel was a wooden wheel that was supported by 12 spokes which fit into a central hub. The combination of the hub and the spokes made the wheel strong enough to carry the family members and their belongings. If the spokes did not fit directly into the hub and went off in different directions, then the wheel would have been considerably weaker and would have collapsed under the weight of the individuals and their possessions.

Your *Business Wagon Wheel* consists of your organization's hub, spokes, and the wheel itself. Your hub is the value your organization is known for delivering to customers. This is what you build everything in your business around. The spokes represent the different ways in which your organization delivers this value to other people. The wheel represents your customers and your potential customers. The stronger and clearer you make your *Business Wagon Wheel*, the more effectively you can compete in your performance category.

If the activities you do in your business today do not support the value your organization is known for delivering or they do a poor job of supporting this value, customers will become disappointed and frustrated and your business will collapse under its own weight. People will be working hard, but their efforts won't be supporting the organization's brand and customers will become confused. To strengthen your brand, make sure every spoke, every activity within your business, connects clearly and effectively to your hub, the value you are known for delivering. Your business will then have the potential to become much stronger.

The Ralph Lauren Hub

On one of the last *Oprah* shows, Oprah Winfrey interviewed Ralph Lauren. As he spoke, I began to realize more and more the hub he built his remarkable business around. He said, "I'm not about fashion. I'm about living. The clothes I've designed and everything I've done is about life, and how people live, and how they want to live, and how they dreamed they would live. That's what I do." On his website, ralphlauren.com, he wrote, "Style is very personal. It has nothing to do with fashion. Fashion is over very quickly. Style is forever."

Keep those statements in mind and then look at his complete body of work over the years including his clothes, his watches, and everything else he has associated his name with. You will quickly see a consistency where each layer from his lowest-cost items to the most expensive all exude his focus on "how people live, how they want to live, and how they dreamed they would live."

Understand Your Current Business

To understand your business as it exists today, answer these questions.

1. What is your business hub? In other words, what is the value your organization is known for delivering to customers?

2. What are the spokes in your *Business Wagon Wheel*? In other words, how does your organization deliver this value?

3. What makes up the wheel for your business? In other words, who are the customers you deliver this value to or the potential customers you could deliver this value to?

Take some time to clarify your business as it exists today. Don't read on. Just pause for several moments to think about your answers to these questions. Until you are absolutely clear about the hub of your business there is no need to start planning for next year or even next month. Without a clear hub, you will start to move into actions that may very well take you all over the board. This will weaken your *Business Wagon Wheel* and lessen your ability to transport your business successfully to profitable growth over the long term.

Conduct a Brand Audit

In order to strengthen your business and increase your chances of gaining a competitive advantage, make a list of all the activities people do in your organization and rank them from the ones that support your hub the best down to the ones that support your hub the least. Then add any other ideas that are not on your list that might connect to your hub even better than the activities you have right now and fit them into your rankings. You will end up with a wide variety of current and potential activities and their relative capacity to strengthen your brand.

Sacrifice to Accelerate

One of my all-time favorite ads was a two-page BMW ad in a magazine. On the left page was a picture of a beautiful car. Above the picture of the car in a great big bold font, it said, "No." At first, I thought this was really odd because I thought the idea was to get customers to look at your product and say, "Yes." On the next page in small print, it essentially said BMW says no to a lot of good ideas so they can say yes to a few great ideas.

I love that. If you try to do every good idea you have for growing your business, how will you have the time, money, and energy to do the few great things that will matter the most? Be willing to let go of a lot of good activities in order to focus on a few great activities that support your hub the best. You define your organization by what you say no to.

After you've ranked all of the activities in your business from those that support your hub the best to the ones that support it the least, I recommend you use a variation of *The 1 – 3 – 6 Process for Focusing Your Efforts* by answering these three questions.

1. What is the value your organization is known for delivering to its customers?

2. What three things happen in your organization or could happen in your organization that support or could support the delivery of this value the best?

3. What six things does your organization need to stop doing or spend a lot less time doing so employees have the time and the energy to do the three things you know will have the greatest positive impact on supporting the value you are known for delivering?

After you have clearly decided on your business hub, really hone your activities down to the few that best support this hub. This is how you can work to intentionally craft your brand the way you want it. This is vastly more effective than trying to do 20 things that are going to eat up a ton of time and money and have little or no impact on strengthening your organization's brand.

Remember Ralph Lauren started with a single tie to build his empire, but with everything he added he stayed true to his hub. Do the few things you've decided to do that fit your hub extremely well, and do them as well as you can. Then gradually add more spokes to your *Business Wagon*

Wheel as you become capable of doing each of them at a very, very high level.

The Operational Responsibilities of Strengthening Your Brand

For every decision you make in any aspect of your business, ask yourself and others, "Is this good for our brand over the long term?" If you do something that helps your short-term numbers and hurts your long-term brand, you will damage the most important asset your organization has going for it. I've learned it takes two years to develop a strong enough brand for a new product or service to be consistently requested by customers. It requires a sustained focused effort to penetrate the minds of your customers and potential customers and to be in their top two choices for any performance category. However, a great brand can be ruined very, very quickly so be discerning in the decisions you make.

Consider Reinventing Your Business

You may reach a point where you decide you need to reinvent your business. There are a variety of reasons why this might happen. First, you might realize there is little or no chance your organization will ever become number one or number two in the performance category you are operating in. Second, you might see that you don't have a sustainable competitive advantage in this type of business and that it's only a matter of time before your organization will fail. Third, you might be number one in the category, but you are not able to generate significant enough profits in this type of business to make it worth the efforts of all the people in your organization.

If you change any or all of the three parts of your *Business Wagon Wheel*, you will reinvent your business. Here are three questions that can guide you on the path to reinvention.

1. What value do you want your organization to be known for delivering that it is not already known for delivering?

2. How do you want to deliver this value that would be different than the way it is being delivered right now?

3. Who do you want to sell that value to other than your current customers and prospects?

If you change the value you deliver to customers, the way you deliver this value, and/or the type of people you deliver the value to, you will have a very different business than the one you have today. This could turn out to be a really great thing for your organization, but before you run off to reinvent your business, here are a few thoughts for you to consider.

Reinventing your business can drive dramatic profitable growth. However, changing any one or all three of these variables will significantly alter your business and your future for better or worse. Changing parts of your *Business Wagon Wheel* repeatedly can destroy your brand and ruin your business. Customers can become very confused and wonder what you stand for. Consider reinvention carefully before you move ahead.

Walt Disney and the Making of a Great Brand

The famous business leader I've studied the most is Walt Disney. He exemplified many of the ideas on branding I've explained so far in this chapter. Here are three books on Disney I recommend: *Walt Disney: The Triumph of the American Imagination* by Neal Gabler, *The Magic Kingdom: Walt Disney and the American Way of Life* by Steven Watts, and *Walt Disney: An American Original* by Bob Thomas.

The original performance category of his company in the 1920s was animated short films. The hub of his business was entertaining moviegoers of all ages before a full-length action film began. He generated additional revenue by selling Mickey Mouse watches. By the mid-1930s, he realized he needed to expand his performance category in order to make reasonable profits so he created full-length animated films beginning with *Snow White* in 1937.

After World War II, he reinvented his business several more times by gradually expanding the ways in which he delivered entertainment to all members of the family. He added live-action films, television shows, and a theme park. His business hub of entertaining all members of the family never changed, but the ways in which he delivered value kept growing. The sustainable competitive advantage of The Walt Disney Company was its ability to keep finding ways to entertain all members of the family. Long after Walt Disney's death, this hub of value was delivered in new ways by The Disney Channel on cable television, several ESPN stations, the ABC television network, Disney.com, espn.com, the addition of many new characters, and new theme parks in Europe and Asia.

Walt Disney provided a great template for every other business to use in strengthening its brand. Define the performance category you are going to compete in and then clarify your business hub, spokes, and wheel, otherwise known as the value you deliver, the ways in which you deliver this value, and the people you deliver this value to. Always stay open to the possibility of reinventing some aspect of your business.

DEPEND ON A CONCEPT, NOT A CUSTOMER

The temptation always exists to land a truly great customer and do whatever the customer wants in order to keep the revenue coming in. The thought process is, "We can't afford to lose this great customer so let's do whatever he or she asks." With no bad intentions whatsoever this great customer keeps asking people in your organization to do all sorts of different things. Before you know it 85% of your revenues are coming from this one customer, and your organization has strayed significantly away from the value it wants to be known for delivering.

There are only two things that can happen at this point. The customer continues to be your customer and the survival of your business grows even more dependent on this customer, or the customer decides to stop buying your products and services and your business collapses dramatically because you have not established the value you want to be known for delivering, potential customers don't know what you have to offer, and you haven't been constantly improving the value you offer. When you go out into the broader marketplace with a weak brand and outdated capabilities, you face a massive challenge.

A Lesson from Apple

In the enormous outpouring of articles and books about Steve Jobs when he died, I think there is one insight that stands out above all the others: he never changed his concept. The concept that governed his two tenures at Apple was, "build electronic devices that are remarkably useful in people's day-to-day lives, make them easy to use, and make them look stunningly attractive."

The Apple II may be extremely primitive compared to today's standards, but at the time it came out it was mind-boggling. I was a freshman in high school in 1977, and my school purchased a few of those computers. I was used to seeing an entire room full of giant machines using punch cards. I was a senior in college in 1984 when the first Macintosh came out. When my classmate down the hallway bought one and I got to borrow it, I thought it was amazingly useful to type an engineering report, save it, and come back later and make corrections. I was the official typist on our team engineering project that year, which might explain why I never actually used my Degree in Mechanical Engineering. I do remember my professor saying I was remarkably fortunate to be on the team I was on. I don't think he meant it as a compliment to me. Obviously from 1997-2011, Steve Jobs stayed true to his concept with the creation of the iMac, iPod, iPhone, iPad, and iCloud.

Be Customer-driven, Not Customer-dependent

The greatest companies in the world are customer-driven, not customer-dependent. McDonald's serves food to millions of people every day. Ray Kroc built his first McDonald's restaurant in 1955. That's a long time of staying true to a single concept: QSC&V. From the very first restaurant to the 14,000-plus restaurants in McDonald's USA, the concept has been to provide quality food with fast, accurate, and friendly service in a clean environment at a reasonable price.

The great companies are driven to always deliver the very best value they can within their concept of value for their customers. However, they are not dependent on the customers in terms of having the customers tell them what to do. If your business is reaching this unhealthy point of being customer-dependent, I encourage you to seriously pause what you are doing and think through the next stage of your business.

Clarify Your Concept

Most importantly, clarify the value you want to be known for delivering. The only way to build a sustainable brand is to consistently deliver the same type of value to all of your customers. Once you've clarified the value you want to be known for delivering, make sure every customer relationship falls under this concept. If you are just doing things to generate short-term revenue, you can easily allow your customers to take you all over the board and then you won't be known for anything. This is a very scary place to be in a highly, highly competitive global marketplace.

Innovate within Your Concept

Once you define the concept of the value you want your organization to be known for delivering over the long term, you are in a great position. You can now effectively innovate every day. Remember that innovation means creating more appropriate value for other people and delivering it through a better experience for them. The problem with innovation is you can literally do hundreds of things for other people that could be of more appropriate value for them, but if you try to do every good idea you come up with then you won't strengthen your organization's brand because a lot of the ideas will fall outside of the concept of value you want to be known for delivering.

Start with your concept. What is the value you want to be known for delivering? Then ask yourself, "Within our concept, how can we create more appropriate value for our customers and deliver it through a better experience for them?"

HOW PROMISES AFFECT BRANDS

Your Brand is Not Your Promise, It's the Customer's Opinion

Some people think a brand is a promise. They are confusing the term "brand" with "brand promise." Your brand is not what you promise to deliver. Your brand is the value your customers and potential customers think you actually deliver in terms of helping them to achieve their desired outcomes.

Having said this, it is critically important you clearly promise your customers what you are going to try to help them to achieve. They need to know what they can expect from you. You can make your promise through a statement on your website, through your advertising, through conversations with customers, through guarantees you put in writing for your customers, and in a variety of other ways. By making a promise, you are taking an active role toward helping to build the brand you want to have. However, no matter how much you promise, your brand is still outside of your control because it is the opinion other people have of your organization. All you can do is make clear promises to your customers and do everything possible to keep those promises.

Since 1998 I've worked with a variety of major brands and one thing they all share in common is they work very hard to communicate a clear promise to their customers and then they work even harder to keep those promises.

Think Through Your Promises

The worst promise is to say, "We have something for everybody." Really? Are you providing the universe? You have to be clear in promising a specific value to a specific group of people. You might attract other customers for other reasons and that's okay, but this won't be the brand you want to build. A clear brand is very powerful because it helps to attract the type of customers you want for the type of value you want to be known for delivering.

Use these three questions as your first set of screens.

1. Did you make a clear promise to your desired customers?

2. Did you keep your promise?

3. Did this promise matter to these types of customers?

If it's not clear what you are promising to improve for your prospective customers, then they may never buy from your organization because they didn't know it could help them.

Another reason they might not buy from you is because they feel you didn't keep your promises in the past. Anytime anyone in your organization fails to deliver on your organization's promise to customers your brand as an organization has been damaged. This is why great brands put a premium on execution. When they do make a mistake, they double down on apologizing and making sure those mistakes don't happen again in the future. This is also why it is so important to conduct regular brand audits. You want to constantly make sure everything you're doing in your organization is helping to deliver on the promises you've made to your customers. Only then can you really optimize your chances for building a great brand.

If they do know what you are promising and people choose not to buy from you, it may be because what you're promising is not relevant enough to them in terms of what they are trying to achieve.

You need to select a performance category that matters to your desired customers. Then you have to be able to deliver a remarkable impact in this category. Then you can make promises to your desired customers. If you steadily perform at a very high level, you can work your way into the number one or number two spot in the minds of your desired customers. When you land in this position, you will have a great brand. Then the key is to keep working to maintain one of those two slots in the minds of your desired customers. If you only reach their third best choice, you will never build a great brand.

McDonald's did this with the McCafe. They found they weren't promising enough to their customers in the area of coffee. Starbuck's was taking away their customers. So McDonald's made a promise to develop high-quality coffee products and delivered on this promise with the McCafe. This has greatly enhanced the McDonald's brand.

The Problems with Promising Too Much or Too Little

This whole business of making promises is serious stuff. If you promise more than you can deliver, you lose credibility quickly and become irrelevant. If you don't promise enough, you may never become relevant. Making a brand promise requires both being realistic and courageous. Here are two questions for you to think through.

1. Can you keep your promise?

2. What else should you be promising?

When Apple shifted from just making personal computers to making iPods, they needed to shift what they could promise delivering, otherwise the music side of their business would have remained unknown. When McDonald's shifted from just food and soda to making the McCafe, they had to expand what they were promising. These two companies couldn't make these promises until they were ready to do so, but once they were ready they had to promise the world that they would truly deliver in these new areas.

The Problem with Changing Your Promises Too Often

A promise is not a marketing slogan or a conference theme. A promise is extremely personal between a company and its customers. Once you promise something to customers, your entire relationship with them rests on your ability to keep this promise. If you keep changing your promises, customers will start to wonder what you really stand for. Just as in a personal relationship, people want to know what you are committed to doing. If you constantly change those commitments, the other person will wonder what kind of a mess he or she has gotten into.

There may come a time when you have to change what you are promising to deliver to your customers. This is how you begin to redefine the brand you want to be known for. However, if you change your desired brand too often, you will end up with the brand no one wants: "They don't know who they are or what they do."

Be very intentional in what you promise to your customers, be sure it matters to them, be sure you can deliver on those promises, and be very careful about changing what you promise.

FEED YOUR BRAND EVERY DAY

A brand is like a person. It needs to be fed every day in order to stay healthy and strong. Take time each day to strengthen your organization's brand. One day you will look back and be amazed by the number of sales you are making to people who come to you wanting to buy your products and services. Here are a dozen ways you can feed your brand every day.

Brand Feeder #1: Carefully Look at What Your Customers See

If your website is the first thing your potential customers see, then study it carefully. Does it clearly explain what business you're in and how you add value to customers? Is it clear what you sell and why those products and services are of value to other people? Is it clear how a person can contact your organization? To be honest, I don't understand companies that make prospective customers fill out an information sheet on the website in order to be called back. Why not just put your phone number and an email address on your website? Why make it hard for people to reach you? Would you have people walk up to your door and tell them to fill out a form and that you might call them back?

If the first interaction a potential customer has with your organization is at a retail location or at an office, does that physical space exude the type of look you want it to project? Does it make the potential customer comfortable or uncomfortable?

You might not be in charge of your website or your facility, but you can at least look at it from the customer's perspective. Then find a convenient time to calmly discuss your observations with whoever is in charge of the website or the facility. Be mature, professional, and tactful, but at least let the person know what you're seeing. If you had a piece of food on your face, would you want someone to pull you aside and tell you?

Brand Feeder #2: Look at How You and Your Staff Interact with Customers and Prospects

Do you and your staff members interact with your customers and prospects in ways that help them to feel respected and supported, or do you laugh at them when they don't know something? One time I got off a flight and ran to the gate for my next flight. The person at the gate laughed at me and said, "That plane has already left." Not exactly a brand-building moment. I've done everything I can not to fly with this company ever again.

Are you patient and pleasant or rushed and rude with your customers and prospects? Feed your brand today by being on the alert as to how you talk with your customers and prospects and make at least one improvement right away. Get your staff members to focus on how they interact with customers and prospects. We all get one chance to make...

Brand Feeder #3: Study the Quality of Your Products and Services and Make One Improvement

When the customer unwraps the new product from your organization and tries it out is he or she happy the first time? Is the person still happy after 50 times or 500 times? Does the person brag to his or her friends about the service from your organization? If not, you will end up with a weaker brand than you could have had.

Brand Feeder #4: Provide Encouragement to your Employees

Your brand exists in the minds of your customers, but it is built through the efforts of your employees. Do they feel encouraged and supported by you to do their very best work? Somewhere down the road your customers are going to be affected directly or indirectly by your employees. Is there a way you can affect your employees today that will increase the chances they will have a positive impact on your customers in the future?

Brand Feeder #5: Do Your Prices Reflect Your Brand Positively or Negatively?

If a person looked at your prices today and compared them to the prices of your competitors, do you feel your current prices would enhance your brand or weaken your brand? Don't be fooled into thinking people always want the cheapest price. They don't. They want an appropriate price. If a Mercedes-Benz salesperson told me I could walk off the lot with a brand-new Mercedes for $14,000, I wouldn't trust him or her. That price doesn't fit the brand. I would believe something was wrong with the car. If someone charged me $24 for a hamburger, I would question what I was doing there. Do you have the appropriate price for the value you want to be known for? Your price can endear a customer to you or make them bewildered.

Brand Feeder #6: Take Social Media Seriously or Not at All

If you say you're going to blog every week or every day, then do it. If you say you're going to post updates on Facebook, then do it. If you say you're going to Twitter away with tips every morning, then do it. Some companies take social media seriously and have dramatically enhanced their brand. Others talk about taking social media seriously and then people question their brand because their social media efforts happen only very sporadically. Either take it seriously, or don't do it.

Brand Feeder #7: Consider What Your Brand Says and What It Does Not Say

The ultimate brand-killer is trying to be something different every day just to close a sale with a different customer every day. No organization is for every pocketbook. You can build a massive company with a very clear brand (Disney: entertain all members of the family; Ralph Lauren: provide the look of the luxury lifestyle; American Girl Doll: in the little girl business), but you can't even build a successful small business without people having a clear understanding of the value you sell. Take time today to look at your brand. How do customers describe the value they receive from your business and what it is like working with your organization? Clarify what your organization stands for and communicate that to your employees, customers, and prospects.

Brand Feeder #8: Send a Personal Touch to a Customer

Rather than wondering what you can do today at work and just filling up your time with busywork, I suggest you pull out a stack of personal note cards and write a handwritten note to 25 customers. If you do that once a quarter, your relationship will be much stronger with each of them. Don't just write the same thing to each person. Make each note personal and unique.

If you don't know your customers because of the role you're in, then write a handwritten note to 25 franchisees or suppliers. The point is you strengthen your organization's brand when you strengthen your relationship with key people associated with your business.

Brand Feeder #9: Look at Your Advertising from Your Customers' Point of View

If your company invests in television, newspaper, online, billboard, email, and/or radio advertising, look at this advertising as though you were a customer or a prospective customer. Does the advertising make sense to you? Is it clear how you would be better off as a result of using that product or service? Does it in some way increase your emotional desire to buy from your organization? Be honest with the people responsible for the advertising. In a professional, one-on-one conversation let the person know what your observations were like. Take ownership of your brand and at least express your opinion. Do so with tact and maturity, but let your thoughts be known.

Brand Feeder #10: Provide Free Value, otherwise known as The Santa Approach

One of my favorite movies on branding is *Miracle on 34th Street*. That's the one where the Santa at Macy's tells the moms where they can buy certain toys that aren't available at Macy's. In other words, Santa gave away free value and instead of losing customers he actually increased customers for Macy's because the moms knew they would get good advice on where to find things. He was like an early version of Google, which also gives away tons of information for free and has built an amazing business.

What value that is relevant to your customers can you give away for free? This is important. People love the opportunity to try out an organization before they commit to a paying relationship. Do you have some type of free value on your website so people can gain a sense of what it is like to work with you? Can you put free advice on your website, can you give away free samples of your product, or can you let your customers try your service for free for 30 days?

Brand Feeder #11: Look at Your Schedule and Make Sure Your Efforts Support the Desired Brand

This is the whole point of this section. Are you really feeding your brand every day in some way, or are the hours in your day being eaten up by stuff that won't enhance your organization's brand at all? Look at your schedule for the rest of today and tomorrow. What specifically will you do to enhance your organization's brand? If you don't have anything on your calendar that is helping the brand, then you better look at what you can take off and what you can put in place to advance your brand in some way. You might decide the one thing you can do today is to let 10 of your friends and family members know more about your company's products and services. If every employee raved about your company to the people he or she knows outside of work, it could be a tremendous step forward toward strengthening your organization's brand.

Brand Feeder #12: Search for Ways to Improve the Operational Aspect of Delivering Value to Your Customers

A brand is built, or ruined, by an organization's ability to consistently and efficiently deliver the value it promised would be delivered. Think of Anheuser-Busch InBev, Toyota, and Wal-Mart. They sell an amazing amount of products every year and yet the consistency and efficiency of their operations are remarkable.

Look at the flow of your organization. From the time a customer requests a certain product or service to the time he or she receives that product or service to all the times he or she uses that product or service is there anything that can be done to improve the consistency and quality of the customer's experience with that product or service? Is there anything that can be done to improve the efficiency with which the value is delivered to the customer? All the marketing in the world doesn't make a brand strong if the delivery of the promised value is poor.

Brand Feeder Bonus: Get Away from Your Work so You Can Come Back with Better Mental Energy

Ironically, you need to stop working some of the time in order to better understand your brand. When you are away from your work, stay away. Give your brain a rest. When you come back to looking at your brand you can do so with fresh eyes. You might just see something obvious that you never saw before.

An Open Letter to Aspiring Great Business Leaders

The world needs you, your country needs you, your organization needs you, your community needs you, and your family needs you to be at your very best.

This isn't just a catchy little motivational phrase. I'm very serious about this. People need you to be at your very best as a business leader. Whether you're 25, 45, 65, or older, organizations need you now more than ever before. Across the globe and in your neighborhood, aspire for greatness as a business leader for the impact you can make more than the paycheck you can earn.

You will, in all probability, be rewarded financially for doing a great job as a business leader, but that won't be enough for you to make the impact you are capable of making. Every great era in history has had people step up to do the noble work necessary to make a lasting difference. This is what we need from you. Realize your impact as a leader can create value for your customers, generate sustainable profitable growth for your organization, help your country get on solid financial footing, make an enormous difference in your community as you volunteer the skills you have developed, and, most of all, enhance the lives of your family members. This commitment to being a great leader in all areas of your life has to be at your peak level, not some derivative effort.

As I look back on my life and my work and the people I've interacted with both personally and professionally, I see patterns of what made some people successful and others not so much. I would like to share some of these lessons with you as you move toward making a greater impact in the world as a business leader.

YOUR PERSONAL FOUNDATION

The impact you have as a business leader over the long term is directly related to the strength of your personal foundation. Here are a few thoughts on strengthening your foundation.

Communication Strength

Do you listen when other people talk? I mean really listen. Do you let them finish their complete thoughts and pause for a moment before sharing your opinions? Are you interested in learning what they believe? When you share your thoughts, do you do so in a way that is clear, concise, caring, and compelling, or do you just dump on other people? Communication is one of the essential skills of leadership. Keep working to communicate more effectively.

Physical Strength

Business leadership requires a lot of energy to stay on top of your game. Eating right and exercising regularly are two of the most important business habits you can develop. Your strength and your cardiovascular fitness will affect your conversations, your stamina, your attention level, and your ability to sustain focus through difficult situations.

Mental Strength

Feed your mind on a regular basis. If great leadership is your ambition, I suggest you consistently read books about great leaders and by great leaders. Make a list of 10 leaders you really admire. These people can be still alive or dead for centuries. Either way, I encourage you to write down their names. Then find at least one book or google for at least one article on each person. Study as much as you can about these people. The insights you gather can be put to practical use in your work.

Moral Strength

I'm not going to tell you what is right and wrong. I do challenge you to clarify for yourself what you believe is right and wrong. On one side of a sheet of paper, write, "Actions I think are the right thing for me to do," and on the other side write, "Actions I think are the wrong thing for me to do." Invest 30 minutes total filling in both sides. Every day for the next three weeks read over both lists and add or delete words until you have the two lists the way you want them.

Then read over those two lists three times a week. I think you will be amazed by how much more you do the little things you think are right and how much less you do the little things you think are wrong. It's sad to see the number of people who reached the pinnacle of success in their chosen field only to crash down because they didn't have the moral strength to do what they had already decided was the right thing to do. It usually started with the little things.

Financial Strength

Spend less than you make. Same goes for your business. Debt is a dangerous deal. Actually spend a lot less than you make. Strengthen your savings every day. Money in the bank is just as healthy as physical or mental strength. One of the biggest mistakes of my business career was thinking I could spend my way to success. I thought if I spent enough money on marketing that at the very least I would always make back what I spent. I loved this thought process so much I not only made this mistake in 2001, but I repeated it in 2005 and 2007. You can't force the market to respond to you, and you can't manufacture happiness by spending. Save your money whenever you can. Get stronger financially. Invest wisely in your life and in your business. Think three times before you spend your money.

THE PRIORITY OF YOUR FAMILY LIFE

15 months after I started my own business in 1998 my first child, Sarah, was born. Several business executives pulled me to the side and said, "Make your family your number one priority, and you will build a successful business. If you put your family last every day, your business may not be around for very long." That was, and is, absolutely great advice.

Clients are great and projects are fun and exciting, but they have short shelf lives. The family you grew up in and the family you may have created are the most important relationships you have. Treat them with the utmost respect. Sometimes business leaders get things backwards. They think the key is to lead a global organization and then share what little crumbs of time they have left with their family. I've learned it's the other way around. If you prove you can do a good job at home, then you have the ability to lead lots of other people. If you aren't loyal and committed to the well-being of your family members, you probably won't have that skill set for your employees either.

THE NECESSITY OF FRIENDS

I'm not talking about going out and partying. I'm talking about the real need to have someone to talk with, someone to exchange ideas with, and someone to discuss your career and family life with. Conversations with your significant other are critically important, but so are conversations with friends, really good friends, the ones who will be honest with you and who will encourage you. These friends can help you be better at home, at work, and in your community. These kinds of friendships require effort and time and patience and being there for each other over the long term.

I have been the enormous beneficiary of two remarkable 35-year friendships. I met Mike Feder and Jeff Hutchison when I was a freshman in high school. We were good friends for about 15 years and then we took things to a higher level. For the next 20 years, Feds, Hutch, and I met for at least three days each year for our Dream Weekend where we discussed what went well the previous year, what didn't go well, and what we dreamed of accomplishing in our lives over the next year both personally and professionally.

Feds was in Kansas City, Hutch was in Chicago, and I was in St. Louis. We had eight kids between the three of us in those 20 years, and we had three very busy careers and lots of community responsibilities. The reason our friendships worked so well was because we worked at them. We made time for each other, we listened to each other, and we challenged each other's decisions and thought processes.

Hutch and I lost Feds to brain cancer three days before his fiftieth birthday on November 24, 2012. He was 24 days younger than me. His example and wise counsel continue to influence Hutch and I in many ways. Hutch and I still turn to each other for advice and perspective and friendship and encouragement and fun, and we still go on our annual Dream Weekend.

It's important to make time for friends in your life.

A COMMITMENT TO YOUR BUSINESS: YOUR PURPOSE, YOUR EMPLOYEES, YOUR CUSTOMERS, YOUR PARTNERS, AND YOUR SUPPLIERS

Bet you thought I was never going to get around to your actual business life. The reason I put your foundation, your family, and your friendships before your professional life is because the most important thing you bring to your business is you. You are made up of your foundation, your family, and your friends. The stronger you are in those areas, the more value you have to bring to your business.

However, you do have to be committed to your business in order to be a truly great business leader. You can't just get to it when you feel like it. Every industry and every business has a vast array of nuances that are critically important. You can only gain real understanding of those nuances by immersing yourself into understanding your business. There are widely differing employee communication needs you will have to meet, there are supplier and business partner concerns for you to address, and there are customers to study in order to provide them with appropriate value. Strategies need to be developed and clarified and communicated, plans need to be executed well, and adjustments need to be made.

If your only reason for working is a paycheck, you may very well never bring the passion necessary to make the impact you are capable of making. You need an underlying purpose for doing the work you are doing. Take the time to identify this purpose and to reflect on it consistently. People need you to be at your very best as a business leader. Great business leaders can dramatically enhance their organizations and the impact those organizations have all over the world.

A COMMITMENT TO YOUR COMMUNITY: LOCALLY, NATIONALLY, AND GLOBALLY

Beyond just your organization, there are so many other people who can benefit from you at your very best. That's a fancy way of saying, "Volunteer. Give your time and energy and talent to impact your local community, national causes, and/or world-wide issues."

Feds created a not-for-profit charitable organization called "Gotta Have HOPE" with his wife, Joyce. They actually started it in 2008, which was three years before Feds found out he had cancer. The organization's objective is to raise money and provide support in multiple ways for a remarkably poor school in Uganda. In time, the hope is to spread the impact beyond Uganda. To me, it was a real-life example of a business leader taking his skills, combining them with the remarkable leadership skills of his spouse, and applying them in a committed way to enhance the world.

FINAL ENCOURAGEMENT

Stay focused every day on bringing the best you have to offer to other people.

Sometimes we wonder if we really matter. We wonder if what we do really matters at all in the big picture of things. The temptation is to stop trying our best and to think there really isn't much of a difference between an average effort and a great effort. I want to clarify for you that your best effort every day really does matter very, very much.

The world needs your best, your country needs your best, your organization needs your best, your community needs your best, and your family needs your best. Please, not just for your sake, but for the sake of other people, bring your very best effort every day to your life as a leader.

ABOUT THE AUTHOR

Dan Coughlin works with business leaders to improve their bottom-line results by impacting teamwork, execution, innovation, and branding. As a keynote speaker, seminar leader, executive coach, and leadership consultant, his clients include McDonald's, Toyota, Marriott, GE, Coca-Cola, St. Louis Cardinals, Anheuser-Busch InBev, RE/MAX, Abbott, Shell, BJC Healthcare, Prudential, Cardinal Health, Kiewit Construction, Boeing, and more than 200 other organizations.

To visit Dan Coughlin's *Free Learning Center on Business Leadership* go to:

www.thecoughlincompany.com